The Revels Plays
COMPANION LIBRARY

E. A. J. HONIGMANN, J. R. MULRYNE
and R. L. SMALLWOOD
general editors

For almost thirty years *The Revels Plays* have offered the most authoritative editions
of Elizabethan and Jacobean plays by authors other than Shakespeare.

The Revels Plays Companion Library
provides a fuller background to the main series by publishing worthwhile dramatic
and non-dramatic material that will be essential for the serious student of the period.

The books in the series fall into main groups:
(1) Editions of plays not included in the main series and less exhaustively annotated.
Usually several plays to a volume either by the same author or on a similar theme.
(2) Editions of significant non-dramatic works: masques, pageants, and the like.
(3) Theatre documents and similar source material.
(4) Criticism: collections of essays or monographs.
(5) Stage histories and eye-witness accounts.

Documents of the Rose Playhouse ed. RUTTER

The court masque ed. LINDLEY

Shakespeare and his contemporaries ed. HONIGMANN

Three Jacobean witchcraft plays ed. CORBIN, SEDGE

John Weever HONIGMANN*

Rare Sir William Davenant EDMOND*

Further titles in active preparation
including THOMAS HEYWOOD *Three marriage plays* ed. MERCHANT

*these titles published in the USA by St. Martin's Press

John Weever

VERA EFFIGIES IOHANNIS WEEVER ÆTATIS SVÆ 55. ANNO 1631.

Lancashire gaue him breath,
And Cambridge education.
His studies are of Death.
Of Heauen his meditation.

John Weever, 1631

THE REVELS PLAYS COMPANION LIBRARY

John Weever

A BIOGRAPHY OF A LITERARY ASSOCIATE
OF SHAKESPEARE AND JONSON, TOGETHER
WITH A PHOTOGRAPHIC FACSIMILE OF
WEEVER'S *Epigrammes* (1599)

E. A. J. HONIGMANN

Manchester University Press

© E. A. J. Honigmann 1987

Published by
Manchester University Press, Oxford Road, Manchester M13 9PL, UK

British Library cataloguing in publication data
Honigmann, E. A. J.
   John Weever: a biography of a literary associate of Shakespeare & Jonson, together with a
   photograph facsimile of Weever's Epigrammes (1599).—(Revels plays companion
   library)
   1. Weever, John—Biography.   2. Poets, English—Early modern, 1500–1700—Biography.
   I. title   II. Weever, John. Epigrammes   III. Series.
   821'.3   PR2384.W75Z/

ISBN 0–7190–2217–7 *hardback*

Printed in Great Britain
at the University Printing House, Oxford

CONTENTS

Plate I from *Ancient Funeral Monuments* (1631), author's copy; Plate II (*a*) and (*c*) by courtesy of the Public Record Office; Plate II (*b*) by courtesy of Queens' College, Cambridge; Plate III by courtesy of the Society of Antiquaries of London.

GENERAL EDITORS' PREFACE

Since the late 1950s the series known as the Revels Plays has provided for students of the English Renaissance drama carefully edited texts of the major Elizabethan and Jacobean plays. The series now includes some of the best known drama of the period and has continued to expand, both within its original field and, to a lesser extent, beyond it, to include some important plays from the earlier Tudor and from the Restoration periods. The Revels Plays Companion Library is intended to further this expansion and to allow for new developments.

The aim of the Companion Library is to provide students of the Elizabethan and Jacobean drama with a fuller sense of its background and context. The series includes volumes of a variety of kinds. Small collections of plays, by a single author or concerned with a single theme and edited in accordance with the principles of textual modernisation of the Revels Plays, offer a wider range of drama than the main series can include. Together with editions of masques, pageants, and the non-dramatic work of Elizabethan and Jacobean playwrights, these volumes make it possible, within the overall Revels enterprise, to examine the achievement of the major dramatists from a broader perspective. Other volumes provide a fuller context for the plays of the period by offering new collections of documentary evidence on Elizabethan theatrical conditions and on the performance of plays during that period and later. A third aim of the series is to offer modern critical interpretation, in the form of collections of essays or of monographs, of the dramatic achievement of the English Renaissance.

So wide a range of material necessarily precludes the standard format and uniform general editorial control which is possible in the original series of Revels Plays. To a considerable extent, therefore, treatment and approach is determined by the needs and intentions of individual volume editors. Within this rather ampler area, however, we hope that the Companion Library maintains the standards of scholarship which have for so long characterised the Revels Plays, and that it offers a useful enlargement of the work of the series in preserving, illuminating, and celebrating the drama of Elizabethan and Jacobean England.

E. A. J. HONIGMANN
J. R. MULRYNE
R. L. SMALLWOOD

PREFACE

John Weever published the first poem addressed to Shakespeare—in 1599—and at the same time wrote admiringly of Jonson and Marston. He participated in the famous Poetomachia of 1599–1601, appears to have been ridiculed by Marston and Dekker as Jonson's hanger-on, and also to have been slapped down by Jonson, whom he had warned against satirical excesses in the Humour plays. In the three years from 1599 Weever published at least five books of poetry, four of them filled with allusions to the London literary scene. Before that he had studied at Cambridge, where he wrote dozens of epigrams about his contemporaries and their teachers – a collection that ranks with *Gesta Grayorum* and the Parnassus plays as a major document of student life in the late Elizabethan age. Shortly before he died he brought out an invaluable antiquarian work, in 1631, which had occupied him for many years – perhaps as many as thirty. He was personally acquainted with the leading poets of his day, and, in his later years, with leading antiquaries and heralds, who helped him with his researches. Despite these important achievements and equally important literary connections, no one has published a biography of Weever, other than the short notice in the *Dictionary of National Biography* and one or two derivative accounts. Weever's twentieth-century editors seem to have been unaware of the two large volumes of his papers in the Library of the Society of Antiquaries, and failed to follow up many clues in the books they consulted: this, therefore, is the first detailed biography of John Weever – one that, in passing, also throws new light on his great contemporaries and on the literary scene of his day.

I have received help from many libraries and individuals, and gratefully acknowledge it. I am indebted to the Bodleian Library for permission to reproduce Weever's *Epigrammes* from the edition of 1599; to the Houghton Library, Harvard University, for permission to collate variants in the only other surviving copy of the *Epigrammes*; and to the Folger Shakespeare Library, for permission to quote from its manuscript copy of *The Whipping of the Satyre*. I am also grateful to the Public Record Office and Queens' College, Cambridge, for allowing me to reproduce Weever's signature; to Mr Iain Wright, Librarian of Queens' College, for generous assistance and advice; and to the Public Record Office for permission to print the wills of John and Anne Weever, and to quote from other documents. The John Rylands Library kindly permitted me to quote from English MS. 213; the College of Arms gave me access to the Vincent Manuscripts, and the Lancashire Record Office and Sir Bernard de Hoghton, Bart., to the de Hoghton archives and to other Lancashire collections. The Society of Antiquaries of London and its Librarian, Mr J. Hopkins, allowed me to study Weever's manuscripts at leisure, to quote extracts from them, and to reproduce Weever's note on Sir Thomas Langton.

In addition I must thank the following for answering my enquiries, and for help of various kinds: Dr Susan Brock, Mr Albert Clayton, Professor W. Craig Ferguson, Sir Bernard de Hoghton, Bart., Mr K. Jensen, the staff of Newcastle University Library, Mrs E. Nixon, Miss Kathleen O'Rawe (who helped most patiently with my typing), the Rev. J. Roberts, Mr and Mrs Ashley Russell, Professor David West, and Miss Susan Willis. I am particularly grateful to Professor Harold Jenkins and Dr Robert Smallwood, who read through my typescript and suggested many corrections and improvements. Also to my wife, for many kinds of correction, and help with proof-reading – and for giving house-room to John Weever, a guest who was invited for a short visit and stayed for some years.

Next, a word of warning. To reduce printing costs I have normally modernised the spelling when quoting from older books and manuscripts, and sometimes in book-titles. Square brackets are used to indicate deletions in extracts from manuscripts but also, now and then, to indicate my editorial insertions. I hope that occasional inconsistencies will not cause confusion.

LIST OF ABBREVIATIONS

The following abbreviations have been used for books, the publications of learned societies, libraries, etc.

BL—The British Library (formerly British Museum).

Chambers, *Elizabethan Stage*—*The Elizabethan Stage*. By E. K. Chambers. 4 vols. Oxford. 1923.

Chambers, *Shakespeare*—*William Shakespeare: A Study of Facts and Problems*. By E. K. Chambers. 2 vols. Oxford. 1930.

Crawford—*see England's Parnassus*.

CS—Chetham Society.

DD (etc.)—Documents in the Lancashire Record Office, Preston.

Dekker—*The Dramatic Works of Thomas Dekker*. Edited by Fredson Bowers. 4 vols. Cambridge. 1953 etc.

DL (etc.)—Duchy of Lancaster records in the Public Record Office.

DNB—*Dictionary of National Biography*.

England's Parnassus—*England's Parnassus*. Compiled by Robert Allot, 1600. Edited by Charles Crawford. Oxford. 1913.

Epigrammes—*Epigrammes in the Oldest Cut and Newest Fashion*. By John Weever (1599). Reprinted ... by R. B. McKerrow. Stratford-upon-Avon. 1911, reissued 1922.

Faunus—*Faunus and Melliflora (1600)*. By John Weever. Edited by A. Davenport (Liverpool Reprints, No. 2). 1948.

Ferguson, *Simmes*—*Valentine Simmes Printer to Drayton, Shakespeare* etc. By W. Craig Ferguson. Charlottesville, Va.: Bibliographical Society of the University of Virginia. 1968.

Funeral Monuments—*Ancient Funerall Monuments*. By John Weever. 1631.

Hall, *Poems*—*The Poems of Joseph Hall*. Edited by Arnold Davenport. (Liverpool English Texts and Studies). 1949, 1969.

Hasler—*The House of Commons 1558–1603*. By P. W. Hasler. Published by HMSO for The History of Parliament Trust. 3 vols. 1981.

HMC—Historical Manuscripts Commission.

Jonson (Everyman)—*The Complete Plays of Ben Jonson*. Introduction by F. E. Schelling. 2 vols. Everyman's Library. n.d.

Jonson (Oxford)—*Ben Jonson*. Edited by C. H. Herford and Percy and Evelyn Simpson. 11 vols. Oxford. 1925–52.

Lost Years—*Shakespeare: the 'lost years'*. By E. A. J. Honigmann. Manchester. 1985.

LRO—Lancashire Record Office, Preston.

M. (*or* McKerrow)—McKerrow, in his edition of Weever's *Epigrammes*.

Marston, *Plays*—*The Plays of John Marston*. Edited by H. Harvey Wood. 3 vols. 1938.

Marston, *Poems*—*The Poems of John Marston*. Edited by Arnold Davenport. (Liverpool English Texts and Studies). 1961.

Martial—*The Epigrams of Martial translated into English prose*. (Bohn's Classical Library.) 1907.

Nashe—*The Works of Thomas Nashe*. Edited by R. B. McKerrow (re-edited by F. P. Wilson). 5 vols. Oxford. 1958.

Newdigate, *Drayton*—*Michael Drayton and his Circle*. By Bernard H. Newdigate. Oxford. 1941.

OED—*The Oxford English Dictionary*. Edited by James A. H. Murray, etc. 13 vols. Oxford. 1933.

Parnassus Plays—*The Three Parnassus Plays 1598–1601*. Edited by J. B. Leishman. 1949.

PCC—Prerogative Court of Canterbury (all PCC wills are in the Public Record Office).

PRO—Public Record Office, London.

Searle—*The History of the Queens' College of St Margaret and St Bernard in the University of Cambridge*. By W. G. Searle. 2 vols. Cambridge. 1867, 1871.

Shakespeare Encyclopaedia—*A Shakespeare Encyclopaedia*. Edited by O. J. Campbell and E. G. Quinn. 1966.

Sh.Q.—*Shakespeare Quarterly*.

SR—*The Stationers' Registers* (cited from *A Transcript of the Registers of the Company of Stationers of London; A.D. 1554–1640*. Edited by Edward Arber. 5 vols. London. Privately printed, 1875, etc.).

STC—*A Short-Title Catalogue of Books Printed in England, Scotland, and Ireland ... 1475–1640*. Compiled by A. W. Pollard and G. R. Redgrave. The Bibliographical Society. 1926 (2nd edition, 2 vols., 1976 and 1986).

Venn—*Alumni Cantabrigienses*. Compiled by John Venn and J. A. Venn. Part I: From the Earliest Times to 1751. 4 vols. Cambridge. 1922–7.

Whipper Pamphlets—*The Whipper Pamphlets (1601)*. Edited by A. Davenport (Liverpool Reprints, Nos. 5, 6). 2 vols. 1951.

Whipping of the Satyre, The—Part I of *The Whipper Pamphlets*.

I

Introduction

◦⟫०⟪◦

Before I attempt to fill the gaps in John Weever's biography from unpublished and other neglected sources, it will be useful to summarise what
is already known. First, the entry in Fuller's *Worthies of England* (1662),
under 'Lancashire':

> John Weever was born at [   ] in this County, bred in Queens' College in
> Cambridge, under Dr John Person his worthy tutor. He was very industrious in
> the study of antiquity, and composed a useful book of *Funeral Monuments*, in
> the Diocese of Canterbury, Rochester, London, and Norwich. He died in
> London in the fifty-sixth year of his age, and was buried in St James, Clerken-
> well, where he appointed this epitaph for himself,
>> Lancashire gave me Breath,   Middlesex gave we (*sic*) Death,
>> And Cambridge Education.   And this Church my Humation.
>>> And Christ to me hath given
>>> A place with him in Heaven.
> The certain date of his death I cannot attain, but by proportion I collect it to
> be about the year of our Lord, 1634.

The epitaph, as printed by Fuller, was possibly copied from Stow's *Survey
of London* (1633).[1] Weever's tutor, we should note in passing, was not
'John Person' but 'Robert Pearson' (*Funeral Monuments*, p. 864). Fuller
apparently did not know that Weever had published several books of
poetry.

For about three hundred years, *Funeral Monuments* remained Weever's
best-known work. There were reprints in 1661 and 1767, but the publishers did not share Weever's desire 'to continue the remembrance of the
defunct to future posterity', and offered no life of the author. Brief
accounts of Weever can be found in printed books and manuscript collections from the seventeenth to the nineteenth centuries; an important one,
in P. Whittle's *History of the Borough of Preston* (Preston, 2 vols., 1837),
appears to have been partly based on local information:

> John Weever ... This learned man was born at Preston, in the county of Lancas-
> ter, (and not at Lancaster as some have asserted) of poor but religious parents:
> by the care of his uncle Thomas, he was enabled to receive an excellent edu-
> cation, afterwards he was sent to Cambridge, but never entered into orders,
> having left the college with some small annuity as a dependency: he fixed his

residence in Clerkenwell, London ... He departed this life at Middlesex, in 1632, aged 56. A monument was erected at the cost of John Skillicorne, armiger of Preston, being his executor ... (II, 198 ff.) .

As I explain below (p. 83), some of Whittle's statements can no longer be verified and others are probably erroneous; nevertheless, Weever's 'uncle Thomas', and his abandoned intention to enter into orders must be taken seriously, and will be referred to again.

The *Dictionary of National Biography* (1882, etc.) published the first really detailed notice of Weever, written by Sidney Lee, who corrected previous errors and added much new information (and also new errors). Here are some extracts:

Weever, John (1576–1632), poet and antiquary, a native of Lancashire, born in 1576, was admitted to Queens' College, Cambridge, as a sizar on 30 April 1594. His tutor was William Covell ... [He] seems to have left the university without a degree.

Retiring to his Lancashire home about 1598, he studied carefully and appreciatively current English literature, and in 1599 he published a volume entitled *Epigrammes* ... A portrait engraved by Thomas Cecil is prefixed, and described the author as twenty-three at the date of publication, 1599 ...

In the early years of the seventeenth century Weever travelled abroad. He visited Liège, Paris, Parma, and Rome, studying literature and archaeology (cf. *Funeral Monuments*, pp. 40, 145, 257, 568). Finally he settled in a large house built by Sir Thomas Chaloner in Clerkenwell Close, and turned his attention exclusively to antiquities.

Several points here call for immediate comment. (1) Weever's BA supplicat was submitted on 16 April 1598, and the grace was conceded on the same day. We may take it that he graduated at this time. (2) There is no evidence that he retired to Lancashire in 1598, but some evidence that he went from Cambridge to London. (3) The 'portrait engraved by Thomas Cecil' is not found in the only copies of the *Epigrammes* that now survive. It looks as if Lee confused *Funeral Monuments* (which included Cecil's engraving of Weever at the age of fifty-five) and the *Epigrammes*. (4) Exactly when Weever travelled abroad is uncertain. Some of his inscriptions from European churches were probably not copied by Weever on the spot, since he acknowledged 'having read the epitaphs of Italy, France, Germany, and other nations, collected and put in print by the pains of Schraderus ... and other foreign writers' ('To the Reader', *Funeral Monuments*).

The first modern edition of any of Weever's books of poetry appeared in 1911.[2] R. B. McKerrow, whose *Thomas Nashe* had already set new standards for the editing of Elizabethan texts, unhappily gave far less time to his edition of Weever's *Epigrammes*:

It was not at first my intention to add any explanatory or illustrative notes ... but there is much in these epigrams which calls insistently for annotation. I have therefore added a few brief notes on the allusions ... and have made an attempt to identify the persons referred to. Unfortunately in several cases I have found this impossible.

The 'persons referred to' later proved to be important clues as to Weever's family and connections. Many new identifications—some certain, some probable—are made in the notes in the Appendix, below.

In the present century one man devoted many years to the study of John Weever and his circle, and advanced knowledge in several ways. Arnold Davenport, of Liverpool University, is probably best known for his valuable editions of *The Collected Poems of Joseph Hall* (Liverpool, 1949) and *The Poems of John Marston* (Liverpool, 1961); at much the same time as these volumes, in which Weever's awareness of his two contemporaries is fully demonstrated, Davenport published editions that will later need more attention, (i) of Weever's *Faunus and Melliflora* (1600) in 1948, and (ii) of *The Whipper Pamphlets* (1601) in 1951. In (i) Davenport's introduction and notes listed Weever's unrecorded allusions to Chaucer and Spenser, and his echoes of *Arcadia*, *Hero and Leander*, *Venus and Adonis* and *Love's Labour's Lost*. The former Cambridge student had clearly given much time to English poets, not least William Shakespeare—a fact of some importance for us when we ponder the identity of 'Ingenioso' (cf. p. 52), the former student who is one of the heroes of *The Return from Parnassus* (*c.* 1600). In (ii) Davenport showed that the first of the three Whipper pamphlets, *The Whipping of the Satyre*, can only be by John Weever, concluding that 'we may, I think, regard the case as proved'. Since *The Whipping* attacked John Marston, Edward Guilpin and Ben Jonson, Davenport's identification of its author ties in neatly with my suggestion, based on entirely different evidence, that Marston and Jonson lampooned Weever in plays and poems at roughly the same time.

The present writer's *Shakespeare: the 'lost years'* (1985) included a chapter on 'John Weever and the Hoghtons', the starting-point for Chapter II below.

No one who has written about Weever in this century appears to have made use of his manuscripts, though they were mentioned in W. T. Lowndes's *The Bibliographer's Manual of English Literature* (1834): 'The original MS. [of *Funeral Monuments*] is in the Library of the Society of· Antiquaries'. The Library's own description, 'original MS. of Weever's Funeral Monuments', seems to have been echoed by Lowndes, but is not accurate: though the two large volumes are in Weever's hand, they are not 'the original MS.' but rather notes and jottings, taken over many years, which were extensively rearranged when Weever prepared the printer's copy. These volumes also contain much unpublished material, some of it autobiographical.

Family connections in Lancashire

◈⟫∘⟪◈

Lancashire gave him breath,
And Cambridge education.
His studies are of death.
Of heaven his meditation.

In his last publication, *Funeral Monuments* (1631), John Weever placed these verses beneath a portrait of himself, engraved by Thomas Cecil, with the legend 'Vera Effigies Iohannis Weever AEtatis Suae 55. Anno 1631.' We know, therefore, that he was born in 1575 or 1576, and that he studied at Cambridge; and that makes it possible to identify him as the 'Ioannes Weaver Lancast.' who was admitted as a sizar at Queens' College, Cambridge, on 30 April 1594. In his first publication, the *Epigrammes* (1599), he had claimed Henry Butler, Esq. as his maternal uncle (iv.1), and had inserted dedications to Sir Richard Hoghton, the High Sheriff of Lancashire, and other members of Sir Richard's influential family. These are the most important clues as to John Weever's early life and, as will emerge, they lead us to unpublished documents that fill some of the gaps in his story.

According to Whittle (cf. p. 1), Weever's parents were 'poor but religious'. In the absence of hard facts about them we must be grateful that their son identified himself as the nephew of Henry Butler, Esq., presumably the most important member of his family. McKerrow, in his edition of the *Epigrammes*, failed to trace Henry Butler, but this has now been done. Henry Butler, Esq., of Rawcliffe, in the parish of St Michaels-on-Wyre, lived not far from Lea Hall, one of Sir Richard Hoghton's residences, and was connected with the Hoghtons in various ways, which no doubt explains why his nephew dedicated his first book to Sir Richard, one of the wealthiest men in Lancashire.[1]

Henry Butler of Rawcliffe is already well known to local historians as a landowner who figures in many records of the late sixteenth and early seventeenth centuries, and, since he had a litigious temper, much more can be learned about him from unpublished sources. The Rev. G. J. Piccope printed Henry Butler's will, dated 20 May 1619, in 1861, with the following useful footnote:

Henry Butler of Rawcliffe Esq. ... married Anne daughter of Henry Banister of Bank Esq. by whom he had issue William his son and heir, Nicholas, Thomas, Robert, Margaret wife of William Haggerston of Haggerston co. Northumberland, Joan wife of John Smith of Stalmin Grange, Prudence wife of Thomas Singleton of Scales, and Gismund who married John Atherton of Atherton Esq.[2]

Piccope transcribed the *copia vera*, not the original parchment will (both survive in the Lancashire Record Office), but his version is reasonably accurate. Here, then, we have a clutch of Weever cousins, who may help one day to identify his parents, and also invaluable facts about Henry Butler's family—yet no hint that the Butlers of Rawcliffe were Catholics, which we know from other records: 'Henry Butler adhered to the religious faith of his ancestors', wrote Henry Fishwick in 1891.[3] 'The vicar of St Michaels sent a report to the Consistory Court at Chester, that he and all his family were recusants.' Adam Wolfenden, vicar of the parish of St Michaels-on-Wyre, certified *c.* 1610 that Anne and Marie Haggerston, aged seventeen and fifteen or so, 'were neither of them in all their lives, to the knowledge of me, the said Adam, at my Parish Church at Divine Service ... or to be catechised'; and the two girls had been brought up by Henry Butler and his wife Anne 'from their tenderest years'. The vicar added 'that all these whose names are subscribed are recusants'; his list includes many of Henry Butler's family and of his servants, but neither Henry's own name nor his wife's. Since Henry and Anne Butler had brought up Anne and Marie as Catholics, the vicar perhaps thought that Henry and Anne were Catholics who 'conformed', i.e. attended church to avoid the heavy fines imposed on non-attenders. Whether practising Catholics or 'conformers', however, the Butlers are unlikely to have shared John Weever's Protestant ardour, so clearly expressed in *Funeral Monuments*: their nephew condemned Catholic 'idolatry and superstition', the 'spiritual fornication' of popery, and seems to have leaned towards Scotland (where religion 'is double-refined, pure and spotless without ceremony, and plain as a pike-staff, without surplice').[4] Since Henry Butler failed to mention John Weever in his will, and Weever referred to none of his Butler cousins in his, church differences may have driven a wedge between the two families after 1599.

At the time of his death, said Fishwick, Henry Butler 'held the manors of Middle Rawcliffe and Out Rawcliffe as of fee; he had there twenty houses, eight cottages, a windmill, a dovecote, thirty gardens, and some 300 acres of land'; he also owned two ferry boats on the river Wyre. 'In Stalmine, Upper Rawcliffe, and elsewhere he owned considerable estates. Shortly before his decease he conveyed certain of his lands, etc., in trust to Richard Mollyneux, Richard Hoghton [two of the dedicatees of Weever's *Epigrammes*], Thomas Tyldesley, and others', for the use of his family.[5]

Henry Butler's *inquisition post mortem* reveals even more clearly how wealthy he was:[6] it names his tenants, describes the boundaries of his lands, refers to his slaughter-houses, chapel, and 'all the new building at the hall of Rawcliffe'. This information can be supplemented by a plan of . Upper Rawcliffe and the surroundings, prepared for a special commission that investigated fishing rights on the river Wyre[7] (Henry Butler frequently went to law to defend his fishing interests), a plan that marks the principal houses, highways, weirs, and so on. Anne Butler, Henry's widow, who died shortly after him, also gives us glimpses of the family's life-style in her will; she bequeathed to her eldest son the great bed 'in the chamber called the lord's chamber' and another great bed 'in the great high chamber'.[8] Henry Butler's house, now a country club, still stands, and there is a stone at the top left-hand corner of the tower of St Michaels church with the arms of the Butler family, the initials 'H. B.' and the date '1611'. The litigant who said of the Butlers of Rawcliffe that they were 'of great living and greatly friended'[9] did not exaggerate the importance of John Weever's uncle.

As I have indicated, Weever seems to have been a poor relation. Henry Butler may have helped by sending him to Cambridge, and by introducing him to the Hoghtons and their circle; after Cambridge, however, Weever had to fend for himself, at least for a while. What more can be learned of Henry Butler's nephew's obscure origins? An unpublished note by Weever, written in or after 1625, sheds new light on his earlier years and gives an unsuspected piquancy to the dedication of the *Epigrammes* to Sir Richard Hoghton.

We have to go back ten years from the publication of the *Epigrammes* to understand the significance of Weever's note, which I give below (p. 7). On 20 November 1589, Thomas Hoghton (the father of Weever's dedicatee, Sir Richard Hoghton) was killed in a night skirmish outside Lea Hall, one of his residences, apparently as a result of disputes about grazing rights. Hoghton had impounded a neighbour's cattle; she, a widow, prevailed on Thomas Langton, known as the baron of Newton and the baron of Walton, to take up her cause—and Langton, with eighty friends and followers, attacked Lea Hall at midnight. Hoghton had only thirty friends and servants to defend him, and, in the darkness, received a mortal wound. Several prominent Lancashire families were involved; the Earl of Derby reported to the Privy Council on 10 December that he had investigated this riot, the Earl's son and heir (Lord Strange) attended the spring assizes in Lancaster for a whole week in 1590, on account of the baron's trial, and the Queen herself sent an angry letter to the justices at Lancaster, forbidding them to give bail to the accused. It was only after protracted negotiations, which may not have been completed until 1605,[10] that the baron and the Hoghtons finally made their peace. Now one of the baron's armed supporters in 1589 was a certain 'Johne Weyver'.[11] An anecdote in *Funeral Monuments* had alerted me to the possibility that he could have been John

Weever's father, and Weever's unpublished note makes this a strong probability. All the more extraordinary, then, that in the *Epigrammes* Weever courted the favour of Sir Richard Hoghton and his friends, and dared to include a poem on the death of Sir Richard's father.

In *Funeral Monuments* (pp. 45–6) Weever recounted a gruesome story about Kelley, the former assistant of the celebrated Dr John Dee: Kelley, 'that famous English alchemist', 'in the Park of Walton in le dale, in the county of Lancaster ... invocated some one of the infernal regiment' to foretell the death of a young gentleman. A corpse was exhumed in a nearby churchyard, and Kelley made it deliver strange predictions. 'I was told this much', wrote Weever, by a servingman, a secondary actor 'in that dismal abhorrid business: and divers gentlemen, and others, are now living in Lancashire to whom he hath related this story. And the gentleman himself (whose memory I am bound to honour) told me a little before his death, of this conjuration by Kelley.' The gentleman whose memory Weever felt bound to honour was almost certainly Thomas Langton, the lord of the manor of Walton le Dale and 'baron of Walton', who numbered a 'Johne Weyver' among his followers in 1589. Here is Weever's hitherto unpublished note concerning Thomas Langton, originally intended for page 497 of *Funeral Monuments*:

> *An oblation or sacrifice to eternal oblivion.*
> Here lies a knight whose name may not be told
> Yet in the book of life it is enrolled.
> And ashy-pale in great fear he doth lie
> Lest these coat-arms should his torn house descry.
> For on his death-bed he desired to have
> An obscure burial, and an unknown grave.
>   He died in the city of Westminster.
>   februar. 20 anno domini 1604.
> Sith then he wished house, name and all suppressed,
> Forgotten now, in God's name let him rest.

... I confess now I keep not the order and method proposed to myself, because this remembrance should have been either altogether forgotten, or else reserved for my other part. But my affection to the dear memory of this party deceased (from whom I do acknowledge to have received many favours) transports me beyond my limits, and makes me commit a further error not answerable, in telling the Reader that the name of him hereunder inhumed (which so unwilling to have his name revealed) was Thomas Langton, Baron of Newton in 'Lanchishyre', commonly called Baron of Walton (another manor ... where he most usually did reside), Knight of the Bath at the coronation of our late sovereign lord King James [well; I know I have transgressed and I desire a favourable pardon *deleted*] a gentleman of many excellent good parts, anciently descended from that renowned, right reverend and graceful family of the Langtons of Church Langton in Leicestershire ... But here, alas, with him the glory of that ancient race lies buried. Well, I know I have transgressed and I desire a favourable pardon.

Some thirty folios earlier, in the same manuscript, there is another draft of this note, with significant variations: 'I confess I come now too near these later times, but my [passionate *inserted*] affection to the dear memory of this party deceased (from whom I do acknowledge to have received many favours) transports me beyond my limits, and makes me (nill I will I) commit a further error ...'[12]

Weever, it seems, was a protégé of Thomas Langton, for whom he felt the strongest affection, and was still in touch with him 'a little before his death' on 20 February 1604 (i.e. 1605; we know the date from other sources). Yet in 1599 Weever dedicated his first book, the *Epigrammes*, to Sir Richard Hoghton, whose influence increased as Langton's declined, since Langton had to surrender to him the manor of Walton le Dale to compensate for the killing of Thomas Hoghton. That, at least, was the end of the affair as described by Edward Baines and other historians of Lancashire.[13] I find, though, in a Chancery suit of 1615 that 'about ten years past' Sir Richard Hoghton purchased from Sir Rowland Lacy and others the manor and lordship of Walton le Dale, paying £12,000.[14] It is known that Langton was in financial difficulties in his later years,[15] so it may be that he paid a fine for Thomas Hoghton's death, and therefore had to sell or mortgage the manor of Walton le Dale, which was later bought by Sir Richard in 1605. (The Lancaster assize records for the period no longer survive.) According to the Preston Quarter Session Records, on 19 April 1605, various gentlemen and others entered 'the Hall of Walton and expelled the possessors ... who held by grant of Sir Thomas Langton, deceased', and on 22 April others, 'all of Newton, forcibly entered the hall and took possession'.[16] We can only guess at the sequence of events, but the 'torn house' of Langton's epitaph evidently referred to the loss of Walton le Dale. The Hoghtons were very much in the ascendant when Weever dedicated his *Epigrammes* to Sir Richard and his brothers-in-law in 1599.

What, then, were the 'many favours' that Weever had received from Thomas Langton? Whittle reports that Weever received an excellent education 'by the care of his uncle Thomas': could this have been Thomas Langton? A memorandum bound in with various Hoghton documents (John Rylands Library, Manchester, English MS. 213) suggests that Langton owed a considerable debt to 'John Weaver', probably the poet's father (cf. p. 6). The memorandum, endorsed 'Will Halton' (probably William Hulton of Hulton, Esq., a close ally of the Hoghtons),[17] gives additional details of the trial of Langton and his followers at Lancaster assizes in 1590. Several dozen men, beginning with Thomas Langton, were indicted for manslaughter, and thirteen (including John Weaver) were charged with murder. Appended is a note, with the heading 'To prove murder', listing some of the facts alleged against the killers of Thomas Hoghton, one being 'the speeches uttered after he was slain, "I am sure he is slain, I have been in his bowels."' We do not know whether John Weaver paid with his life; Thomas Langton, at any rate, did not escape scot-free, and therefore we must assume that those charged with murder were either executed or imprisoned. Young John Weever, the later poet, would have been thirteen or fourteen at the time, and only proceeded to Cambridge five years later. Now, in 1589, or in 1594 it would have been the right moment for Thomas Langton to step in and help John Weever to continue his education.

In Weever's *Epigrammes*, Thomas Langton received no complimentary verses, but his presence still makes itself felt. The 'heart-breaking groans and howling misery' for the untimely death of Thomas Hoghton, Esq. (vi.3) partly refer to Langton, Hoghton's unlucky opponent. Langton himself had married a daughter of Sir John Savage of Rock Savage and of his wife, the Lady Elizabeth Manners, a daughter of the Earl of Rutland—hence, perhaps, the epigram on Roger Manners, the fifth Earl of Rutland (i.13). The wife of Edward Manners, the third Earl of Rutland (the uncle of the fifth Earl), was Isabel Holcroft, the sister of Thomas Holcroft of Vale Royal (see v.16). And the fact that Langton's grandmother was the daughter of Sir Edward Stanley, Lord Monteagle, probably explains why Weever also addressed Lord Monteagle (iii.3).

Weever's Lancashire background is unmistakable in the *Epigrammes*. Of the potential patrons addressed in dedicatory epistles or poems, by far the largest group consisted of Lancastrians, or of men closely associated with Lancashire or Cheshire. (The two counties were linked as the diocese of the Bishop of Chester, and many northern families had estates in both.) The volume was dedicated to Sir Richard Hoghton of Hoghton Tower, High Sheriff of Lancashire, and three of the seven 'weeks' were dedicated to Sir Richard's three brothers-in-law, Sir Thomas Gerard, Sir Peter Leigh and Sir Richard Molyneux; in addition three other dedicatees (Robert Dalton, Esq., Sir Cuthbert Halsall, and Sir Edward Warren) were Lancashire men or landowners and near neighbours of Henry Butler, Esq., Weever's uncle. Lower down the social scale, Weever wrote epigrams for William Hoghton, Sir Richard's brother (vi.4); for two Lancashire clergy-cluded two poems on the death of Ferdinando Stanley, the fifth Earl, who Halton (vi.24)); for his former tutor, William Covell, a Lancastrian and future clergyman (iii.22); and, last but not least for his uncle, Henry Butler (iv.1).

For the best part of a century the Earl of Derby's family had been the dominant one in Lancashire. Weever of course was aware of it; he included two poems on the death of Ferdinand Stanley, the fifth Earl, who had died in suspicious circumstances in 1594 (vi.9, 10). Oddly, though, he did not address one to Ferdinando's brother, William Stanley, the sixth Earl—which is all the more surprising when one learns that Weever seems to have been interested in writing for the theatre (cf. p. 18), and that at the

very time when he was preparing the *Epigrammes* for the press the sixth
Earl was reputedly 'busy penning comedies for the common players'.[18]
Nevertheless, other members of the Stanley circle received tributes—Lord
Monteagle (iii.3), and the Earl of Cumberland (v.9), whose half-sister was
the mother of the fifth and sixth Earls of Derby. The explanation of this
silence may lie in the two poems (v.23, vii.11) written for Thomas and
John Egerton, the sons of Lord Chancellor Ellesmere. The widow of
Ferdinando, the fifth Earl, quarrelled with her brother-in-law, the sixth
Earl, about the Stanley inheritance, and the legal battles waged by the
dowager countess and her daughters against the sixth Earl dragged on for
years; in 1600, however, Ferdinando's widow married the Lord Chancellor, and it was arranged that her daughter should marry Lord
Ellesmere's son, John. It may be that Weever felt that he had to choose
between the two factions, either the dowager countess or the sixth Earl.

By 1599 two more dangerous factions had formed at Queen Elizabeth's
court, one led by the Earl of Essex, the other by his enemies, Sir Robert
Cecil, Lord Cobham and the Lord Admiral. It is interesting that so many
of those praised by Weever in the *Epigrammes* were also supporters of
Essex; some were knighted by him and/or accompanied him on his Irish
campaign in 1599, and must have been absent from England, or very
recently returned, when Weever handed over the manuscript of his first
book to the printer. These Essex supporters included the Earl of Rutland,
Lord Monteagle, Sir Thomas and John Egerton, and at least three of the
'dedicatees' of the *Epigrammes*, Sir Thomas Gerard, Sir Cuthbert Halsall
and Sir Edward Warren.

Apart from Ferdinando, the fifth Earl of Derby, other long dead worthies were also remembered in the *Epigrammes*. We have seen that Weever
had special reasons for alluding to the unfortunate killing of Thomas
Hoghton, Esq. in 1589 (vi.3), but why praise Robert Shute, a judge of the
Queen's Bench who had died in 1590? The answer may be that Shute had
been one of the chief justices at Lancaster;[19] Weever's family probably
knew him in the 1580s—the epigram, in short, did not come from a
complete stranger. In these three instances, it will be observed, Weever
also addressed poems to surviving members of the same family, all with
Lancashire connections.

All the evidence agrees that Weever came from a needy background and
depended, at any rate in his younger years, on friends and patrons. As a
sizar at Cambridge he belonged to the poorest class of students (a sizar
received free food and drink, and performed some of the duties of a college
servant), and after he arrived in London he still needed the support of
wealthier men. His Cambridge college, we may note in passing, had many
Lancashire connections, and his first tutor there, William Covell, was a
Lancashire man. As a young writer he continued to court the patronage of
Lancashire men—Sir Richard Hoghton and his friends (*Epigrammes*,

1599), Edward Stanley of Winwick, Esq. (*Faunus and Melliflora*, 1600), Richard Dalton of Pilling and William Covell (*The Mirror of Martyrs*, 1601). We know that he continued to visit Lancashire, even though he finally settled in London; and the verses printed with his portrait in *Funeral Monuments* prove that he remained proud of his Lancashire origins to the end.

III

Cambridge

∾∘∽

One of the most interesting features of McKerrow's edition of the *Epigrammes* is that he was able to identify many of those named in the volume as Weever's contemporaries at Cambridge. Some, indeed, were contemporaries in his own college: Edmund Gurney (author of complimentary verses; matriculated 1594); William Covell (iii.22; 'Weever's tutor'); George Meriton and George Mountain (iv.19; Fellows of Queens' from 1589 and 1592); and Nathaniel Fletcher (v.10; Fellow of Queens' from 1594). Weever's contemporaries at other colleges included M. Milward (author of complimentary verses. 'Possibly Matthias Milward, a scholar of St John's'); John Overall (iii.23; Regius Professor of Divinity from 1596); Thomas Playfere (iv.13; Lady Margaret Professor of Divinity from 1596); Robert Shute (iv.16; matriculated from Christ's 'in 1598'); William Rich (vi.22; of Pembroke Hall; elected proctor, 1598). In addition, McKerrow referred to the *Dictionary of National Biography* for other Cambridge men, most of whom turn out again to have been Weever's contemporaries in the university: Dr Palmer (ii.11); Lord Monteagle (iii.3); Robert Allott and Christopher Middleton (iv.4), and Dudley North (iv.20).

As my notes on the *Epigrammes* will show, more of Weever's named friends can be identified. Thomas Kedgewin, Gent., who wrote complimentary verses, matriculated at Emmanuel in 1594; Thomas Oxburgh (iv.5) was a pensioner at Queens' from 1594. Richard Upcher, Esq. (ii.16) was almost certainly related by marriage to Dr Humphrey Tyndall, President of Queens' (1579–1614), whose sister married Edward Upcher of Soham; and John Upcher (iv.3) must be a former pensioner of Queens', who matriculated in 1582. The fact that so many of those identified by name were Weever's contemporaries or near-contemporaries, or were members of his college, prompts one to ask whether some of the 'joke' names might allude to other Cambridge figures and, checking through Venn's *Alumni Cantabrigienses*, I was startled by the large number of possible puns. To begin with Queens' College, Weever addressed 'straight' verses to W. Covell, T. Oxburgh, G. Meriton, G. Mountain, N. Fletcher, all members of the college, to Roger Manners and the two Upchers, also connected with the college, while E. Gurney addressed verses to Weever (A4b). One is therefore tempted to unriddle other names as follows: Monoceros (i.15), T. Horne; Gullio (ii.21), J. Gouldson; 'De Ore' (iii.10), J. Oraford; Rodering (iii.13), J. Rodeknight; Dacon (iv.2), G. Deacon; Gnidus (iv.14), S. Nettles (*cnide, gnide*: a nettle); Rudio (iv.21), R. Rudd; Iscus (v.4), J. Isham; Galbus (v.13), H. Gale; Naevius (v.15), C. Nevell. (See also ii.2, 17, 18; iii.5; v.14; vi.6; vii.8.)[1]

If the 'joke' names were aimed at identifiable Cambridge men, it may be that Weever concentrated his wit on the colleges where he had friends, for whose benefit the epigrams were doubtlessly written in the first instance. He addressed 'straight' epigrams to two Fellows at St John's (Dr Palmer and Dr Playfere), to two friends who were probably at St John's (R. Allott and C. Middleton), and M. Milward of the same college wrote complimentary verses for the *Epigrammes*, so the following are probably shafts directed at St John's: Crassus (i.5), W. Crashaw; Palmo (iv.8), J. Viney; Steron (iv.10), J. Stearne; Charis (v.5), J. Grace; 'the cooks' (vi.21), T. Cooke; Lacus (vii.7), H. Lake. At Trinity he praised Dr Overall and Dudley North; I suggest these veiled allusions to other Trinity men: Poenus (i.16), W. Penny; Felix (i.17), N. Gladman; 'spurius scriptor' (iv.11), J. or P. Spurling; Hugo, Chypus, Claius, Boscus (vii.5,6), T. Hughes, H. Chipperfield, S. Claiton, and J. Wood or S. Bush; Cordred (vii.14), R. Stringer.

Many other identifications of 'joke' names are attempted in my notes. Quite often, of course, more than one student's name will suggest itself—for example, Calvus (ii.17), T. Baldwin or D. Wigmore; Ramists (iii.5), R. Lambkin or T. Ram; Cacus (vii.10), F. or J. Cacott—and this should not surprise us. Satirists, partly to protect themselves, have usually claimed that they are not concerned with individuals and have deliberately left some confusing clues. The fact that here and there we are uncertain about the target is less significant than that so often there could be no possibility of doubt. We have to remember, too, that Weever's Cambridge friends would spot the allusion because he referred to a recognisable event, or characteristic; the joke name simply gave one more clue. It goes without saying that the more such 'joke' names one decodes, the more one expects to find. Because there are so many thinly veiled allusions to known Cambridge figures—as well as open allusions to others—the reader naturally assumes that other 'joke' epigrams are targeted on individuals.

Some of the suggested identifications of 'joke' names can only be regarded as tentative, of course; most of the names, however, were invented by Weever, not borrowed from Martial, and, as they occur in a volume that also addresses so many epigrams to quite unmistakable Cambridge figures, one wonders why he coined these particular names. Weever had a marked weakness for punning on names, manifest throughout his *Epigrammes*; so many of the 'joke' names being so similar to the names of his

Cambridge contemporaries, we are justified in concluding that much of the volume—as its tone suggests—consists of undergraduate humour aimed at other students.

We may assume that some of Weever's victims in the 'joke' epigrams could also have been townsmen and college servants, traditional butts who are now less easy to identify than fellow-students. And it should not surprise us to find that a poet who risked antagonising a good number of his coevals also dared to ridicule the university's proctors, even though he actually praised two men who served in this capacity (George Meriton, 1594–5, iv.19; William Rich, 1598–9, vi.22). At any rate, Weever's willingness 'not to please the cooks' (vi.21) looks like a gibe at Thomas Cooke of St John's who, as proctor in 1595–6, could make an unruly student feel the weight of his disapproval; unless there were other epigram-writers at Cambridge who did not 'approve', there is a forced analogy here, best explained as dictated by a pun. And the four epigrams on the moon and the man in the moon (iii.1,4–6) are surely again aimed at an individual, 'crabbed, dry and dogged', perhaps a divine ('He spied a knave in moon all clothed in black'). McKerrow's note on 'Ramists defend in moon to be a man' (iii.5), viz. 'I can find no authority for this nonsensical statement about the Ramists', takes Weever too seriously: all he meant was that 'inside crabbed "moon" there is a real man who pisses, etc.'. The allusion in this epigram to four years of rainy weather dates it fairly precisely, since it is known that the rains which began in March 1594 led to bad harvests for several seasons;[2] the date, then, is 1597 or 1598, and in 1597–8 one of the two proctors at Cambridge was William Moone of St Catherine's, later (1604) vicar of Ridgwell in Essex.

Already at Cambridge Weever seems to have been as combative as he was later to show himself in London, where he quickly made himself known as a colourful character and participated vigorously in the Poetomachia. Whether or not I have correctly identified all the victims of his wit, there can be no doubt that his humour was not always generalised. McKerrow's note on Rodering, 'probably a real person', could and should be attached to dozens of other sarcastic epigrams where, as I have said, the anecdote and 'joke' name together single out an individual who must have been easily recognised. The *Epigrammes*, in short, rival the better-known Parnassus plays as a celebration of contemporary Cambridge, and belong to the same tradition; it is consequently not so surprising that Ingenioso, one of the heroes of *The Return from Parnassus* (*c.* 1600), may well represent John Weever, a recent student who had already flexed his literary muscles while at Cambridge and who, it seems, sought and loved publicity.[3] But the *Epigrammes* are even more revealing than the Parnassus plays, since they are not merely satirical. Weever gives us the two sides of Cambridge life: the ambitious student who tries to please his superiors, and the witty student who claims a leading place among his contemporaries by slapping down the false pretensions around him. The mixture of respectfulness (overdone, but seriously intended) and impudence gives a rounded view of Cambridge—and of John Weever at the crossroads, hesitating between two possible careers.

As I shall explain shortly, a few of the epigrams must have been written after Weever left Cambridge. The majority, though, date from his undergraduate years, and, I imagine, were first recited at some college festivity or simply passed round among friends. How much is original Weever and how much really Martial? The epigrams being so heavily influenced by Martial and his imitators, some readers may feel that their satire should not be regarded as local and topical; Weever, they will say, was an inexperienced poet who echoed his predecessors and really had nothing new to say. Now it is true that many of Weever's verses pick up Martial's themes, repeating his attacks on overdressed fops, false friends, extravagant banquets, mean hosts, whores, critics, other poets, etc., and strike us as derivative; the novelty, in Weever's collection, lies in the fact that harmless translations from Martial serve as a protective cover for other epigrams that are sharply pointed at individuals.

Only one of Weever's epigrams is an acknowledged translation —'*Translat. ex Martial.* / Sabidi, I love thee not, nor why I wot, / But this I wot, Sabidi I love thee not' (iii.20). This is close to the original, as can be seen from the prose translation in Bohn's Classical Library—'I do not love thee, Sabidius, nor can I say why: I can only say this, I do not love thee' (i.32). Three more are almost equally unoriginal; one of the three (ii.14) retains Martial's heading and perhaps carried no contemporary sting.

> *Ad Philerotem.*
> A great demesne, friend Phileros, you have,
> And seven wives all lying in their grave.
> But yet the churchyard far more profit yields
> Than all the revenues of your fairest fields.

Compare Martial, x.43: '*To Phileros.* Your seventh wife, Phileros, is now being buried in your field. No man's field brings him greater profit than yours, Phileros.' What, then, are we to make of v.15, where Martial's Naevia becomes 'Naevius'?

> Great Naevius still bids many unto meat,
> His meat is raw, that no man can it eat;
> All in a chafe, finds fault and strikes the cook
> That to his meat he did no better look.
> Yet this poor cook is in no fault I know,
> For certes Naevius bade him roast it raw.

Compare Martial, iii.13: 'While you refuse to cut up the hare, Naevia, and the mullet, and spare the boar which is already more than putrid, you accuse and ill-treat your cook, on the pretence that he has served up everything raw and indigestible. At such a banquet I shall never suffer from indigestion.' I have already mentioned that one of Weever's contemporaries at Queens' was the son of a lord; as this was not a college where lords were thick on the ground, we may take it as certain that Naevia became 'great Naevius' because Weever had a bone to pick with Christopher Nevell, the son of Lord Abergavenny. And why was Martial's epigram *On Philaenis* reassigned to Mella? 'From one eye always Mella's tears do fall/And what's the cause? She hath but one in all' (v.20); compare Martial—'Philaenis is always weeping with one eye. Do you ask how that can be? She has but one' (iv.65). 'Mella'—not found in Martial—probably puns on the name of a lady known to some of Weever's friends.

It appears, then, that despite one's initial impression that Weever lashed out at the world at large, a high proportion of the satirical epigrams dealt with life and individuals at Cambridge. He adopted some of Martial's themes, but more often than not for a local effect. Martial ridiculed the inhospitable host:[4] when Weever wrote in similar vein of great Naevius or Iscus (v.4) we are initially inclined to think of his verses as general satire; once it is pointed out that Christopher Nevell and John Isham were fellow-students with Weever at Queens' (the first a Fellow Commoner, the second a pensioner, i.e. considerably better off than Weever, a sizar), a different explanation is necessary. Wishing to 'needle' someone known to his friends, the young poet selected a characteristic or recent event reminiscent of Martial, thus magnifying his victim's meanness, or other fault, by placing it in a tradition that stretches back for centuries. Forget the tradition and the epigram on Iscus is a poor thing:

> Iscus, invite your friends unto good cheer
> When they before invited are you hear:
> But else invite them not in one whole year.

Weever, however, squeezed a double insult into his three lines. Isham's 'good cheer', we are left to infer, had it been forthcoming, would still have been on a more modest scale than the banquets of mullet, wild boar, etc., promised by Martial's reluctant hosts, with which they are implicitly compared.[5]

Similarly, the epigrams concerned with whoring, cuckolding, extravagant clothes and bad poets—all themes that go back to Martial—appear to be swipes at individuals, who would be recognised by their Cambridge contemporaries. Again, someone stole Weever's 'little tale of Troy', and, being asked for it, 'all in a fume,/'Twixt two big jaws did wholly it consume' (vi.15): this is not likely to have happened more than once. Someone bends his shoulders, when playing bowls, the way he wants the bowl to run (i.11): evidently a personal mannerism. Someone criticised Weever's prepositions ('The wise grammarian reprehends my muse / Which *in* for praiseful epigrams doth use', iv.3 b): why worry over such a point, unless the poet had been charged as he claimed? 'One of my friends' tipped him off, meeting Weever in Sheep's Green (in Cambridge), that his epigrams are being printed (i.7): the friend was mistaken, but we need not doubt that Weever referred to a real encounter. The last two examples, incidentally, show that the epigrams were known to Weever's contemporaries before they were published, and there are others that imply this as well. Without multiplying instances we may conclude that the *Epigrammes* give us a convincing picture of Cambridge in the 1590s—of the students' jokes and jealousies, their favourite authors and other intellectual preoccupations, and of their relations with tutors, proctors and professors.

A word now about Weever's first tutor, William Covell. A year after Weever's arrival in Cambridge, Covell got into trouble with the authorities because of his 'Puritan' fervour:

> It was in the month of December [1595], that one Covell, Fellow of Queens' College, preached a sermon at St Mary's that created him some trouble before the Vice-Chancellor or the Ecclesiastical Commission. His text was 'My house is the house of prayer, but ye have made it a den of thieves', whereupon he took occasion to rave and inveigh against those that did *Facere speluncam Latronum* of the church, offensively and extraordinarily; charging the noblemen of this realm especially, and in sort also the bishops; in spoiling he meant, the church in the revenues thereof, and alienating its patrimony.

The Vice-Chancellor reported Covell to the Chancellor and to the Archbishop of Canterbury. Whitgift left it to the Vice-Chancellor to admonish Covell to forbear such 'slanderous imputations hereafter. But it seems Covell was somewhat obstinate to make any submission, or acknowledge a fault'; the Vice-Chancellor urged him to make a voluntary public submission, 'which he could not yet induce him to do'.[6] This story is interesting, for the *Epigrammes* not only assure Covell that 'twixt thy lips divinity doth fall/Like beryl drops' (iii.22), they also clearly sympathise with his reforming zeal: Matho, who buys and sells church livings, 'and now hath got three livings at one lurch' (iv.4), has much in common with those who were criticised by Covell. (It was a dangerous position to take for an impoverished sizar of Queens', or a Fellow, for the college President, Dr Humphrey Tyndall, was a noted collector of livings.) Weever, however, also attacked the Puritans (v.19: '*In Vulpem puritanum*'), whose 'lavish-tongued precism will not spare/The chiefest pillars of our clergymen' (*our* clergymen is revealing). I think that he must have meant extreme Puritans, who believed that reform from within the established church was not possible, since he praised others apart from Covell who belonged to the 'reforming' wing of the Church of England.

Covell mellowed in later years and became an apologist of the Church of England. In *A Just and Temperate Defence of the Five Books of Ecclesiastical Policy* (1603) he claimed that Calvin 'was, as Master Hooker termeth him, the wisest man incomparably, that ever the French church did enjoy', but refused to allow 'that it was wholly unlawful, in anything to dissent from him' (p. 133); a year later, in *A Modest and Reasonable Examination*, he defended bishops and archbishops, and even non-residency and 'pluralism', which 'are not against law' (p. 173), even though sometimes abused by idle or covetous clergymen. Weever, I think, remained more consistently 'Puritan' in outlook; as a student he shared Covell's earlier indignation that the Church had been turned into a den of thieves, and thirty years later the same flame still burned in *Funeral Monuments*, where he praised the reformation of the Church of Scotland.[7]

Could it have been Covell who introduced Weever to the works of Shakespeare? An epistle in *Polimanteia* (1595) signed W. C., thought to be Covell, praised 'sweet Cambridge' and several popular poets and poems—'divine Spenser', 'dearly-beloved *Delia*' and other works by Daniel, adding in the margin 'All praiseworthy. Lucrecia Sweet Shakspeare. Eloquent Gaveston. Wanton Adonis. Watson's heir.' This is one of the first printed allusions to Shakespeare's poems, which had been published in 1593 and 1594, and occurs in a book on 'the means lawful and unlawful to judge of the fall of a commonwealth'. It could be, though, that this is a case of the teacher taught—that Weever told Covell about Shakespeare, not the other way round. Weever, even if only a poor relation of Henry Butler of Rawcliffe, knew the Hoghtons of Hoghton Tower and their circle, as we learn from his *Epigrammes*; and Alexander Hoghton, Esq., Sir Richard Hoghton's uncle and a previous owner of Hoghton Tower, had referred to a 'William Shakeshafte' in a section of his will, in 1581, that dealt with his players and 'play clothes'. As I have explained elsewhere,[8] Shakeshafte may well have been William Shakespeare; according to Sir Bernard de Hoghton, a descendant of Sir Richard and the present owner of Hoghton Tower, there is a family tradition, handed down from father to son, that Shakespeare worked for the family in his youth. We cannot regard this account of the dramatist's 'lost years' as established beyond all possible doubt; we need more information—but it is fascinating that, a year after Weever's arrival in Cambridge, his tutor praised Shakespeare, a newcomer on the literary scene, and that Covell, like Weever, was a Lancashire man and, we may assume, would be interested in Lancashire gossip.

The *Epigrammes* also reveal that, while at Cambridge, Weever hesitated between two possible careers. One was literary, both the theatre and poetry being favourite topics in his first book. As regards the theatre, he applauded the achievements of Michael Drayton (i.23), William Shakespeare (iv.22), Edward Alleyn (iv.23), Jonson and Marston (vi.11), and of two Cambridge Fellows who excelled in a performance of *Laelia* (iv.19). He also referred to specific events at a theatre, or to theatre-going generally: Ruffinus 'lost his tongue on stage', 'spits it out' and 'told the people he had none' (ii.6,7); a pickpocket carried away forty-four pounds from a play-house (ii.15); a lurcher proclaimed 'that he had courted at the play his whore' (ii.20); 'Eripha, that old trot, every day/Wafts o'er the water for to see a play' (iv.9); and feathered Tubrio, returning by boat across the Thames, has probably been to the theatre as well (vii.13). Weever also praised poets not connected (in 1599) with the professional theatre (Daniel, vi.10; Warner, vi.13; Spenser, vi.23), and friends of whose literary projects he was no doubt aware (Allott and Middleton, iv.4); further, he frequently ridiculed the pretensions of bad poets (i.8, 18, 21; ii.12–13, etc.)—therefore we may deduce that a career as a writer, and in particular as a writer for the theatre, was considered at this time. The fact that Weever published at least five books of poetry from 1599 to 1601, and seems to have been well known in London's theatrical world in these years, confirms the impression given by his *Epigrammes* and, incidentally, adds weight to the suggestion (cf. p. 53) that he figured significantly in at least one of the Parnassus plays.

Secondly, he evidently thought about a career in the Church. Whittle referred to this possibility ('he was sent to Cambridge, but never entered into orders': cf. p. 1), as he himself did in the epigram addressed to the vicar of Lancaster, Henry Porter: 'Porter, I durst not mell [meddle] with sacred writ ... ' (v.24). The large number of flattering epigrams addressed to leading churchmen, and to Cambridge Fellows who were bound to take the same road to preferment, leads us to suspect that he had similar ambitions (Dr Palmer, ii.2; William Covell, iii.22; Dr Overall and Dr Whittaker, iii.23; Dr Playfere, iv.13; G. Meriton and G. Mountain, iv.19; H. Porter, v.24; W. Rich, vi.22). While there is no record that he was ever ordained, his almost lifelong pursuit of funeral monuments kept him closely in touch with churches, and proves that his interest in the Church was not merely self-seeking. Many of the epigrams hit out at the hypocrisies or abuses of churchmen, whereas the other professions are let off lightly—this also indicates how the young poet's mind was preoccupied at this time. A man 'all clothed in black' may be a knave, and so will 'come no nearer heaven' (iii.4); Rodering, though the owner of a splendid beard, is 'no good divine' for, despite his 'bushy sign', which normally means 'wine for sale', as a purveyor of God's word he 'is but a grapeless, dead, dry vine' (iii.13–14); Sutor Faber has exchanged 'a rapier for a bible', the Spanish fashion 'graceth his holy face', and his new, expensive tastes show that he 'deceived us all' (iv.6); Matho, who trades in deaneries and church-livings, is a 'piller' (despoiler) of the Church (iv.14); a puritanical fox, who castigated 'our clergymen', had to 'crave their friendship' when in trouble (v.19); golden priests were once content with wooden chalices, but 'now golden chalices we make' for 'wooden priests' (vii.9); Cordred impudently begs a living, calling himself 'one of rare parts' (vii.14). Denouncing religious hypocrites, Weever implicitly claims to be different, and, with so many poems on churchmen and their affairs, makes it known that he aspires to join their ranks. These hopes survived until 1601, and perhaps longer. The Church, however, did not offer any immediate prospects and the young poet set off for London, following other 'university wits' who had recently taken the same precarious road to fortune—or, as happened too often, to hack-work, destitution and the debtor's prison.

IV

Early years in London

●◐○◑◐

When did Weever leave Cambridge and settle in London? He probably took his degree in April 1598 (cf. p. 2); according to McKerrow, he was a student from 1594 to about 1598 and 'is supposed, on leaving the University, to have returned to his Lancashire home and to have there spent the next few years'.[1] As I shall show, it is much more likely that he moved from Cambridge to London, where he seems to have been a well-known figure in literary circles until 1601. Then he suddenly disappears from our view, though we know that he was back in Lancashire 'in the beginning of the reign of King James';[2] this could have been either a brief visit or one lasting 'the next few years' after 1601.

To suppose that Weever left Cambridge in or around April 1598 seems reasonable enough. If I am correct in thinking that the four sour epigrams on the moon and the man in the moon refer to William Moone, one of the two proctors at Cambridge in 1597–8 (cf. p. 14), we probably owe the sarcasm about the proctor's dogged nature to an undergraduate who had fallen foul of authority. On the other hand, a complimentary epigram on a proctor could have been written by a former student who wished to keep in touch with influential Cambridge acquaintances, as Weever clearly did (cf. p. 77), so vi.22, 'In Gulielmum Rich: Cantabr. procu.' is less significant for our purposes. Rich served as proctor in 1598–9.

Whenever he arrived in London, Weever had literary ambitions; he brought with him his book of *Epigrammes*, which was published after several delays in 1599, and perhaps too some of the fragments that were included in *Faunus and Melliflora* (1600). He found, as many an aspiring poet has found since, that the world was very willing not to read him—in short, that he had to cultivate friends before he could hope for recognition. The many poems in praise of living poets inserted in the *Epigrammes* were probably a hit-and-miss campaign; some of these eminent contemporaries he may have known personally, but some must have been strangers, and Weever no doubt hoped that a little of the praise that he let fly in all directions would return with interest.

We can piece together the jigsaw of his more meaningful literary friendships by starting with the authors he addressed in commendatory verses.

In 1599 he contributed two sets of verses to Henry Buttes's *Dyet's dry dinner*, and in 1600 two more to Christopher Middleton's *The Legend of Humphrey Duke of Glocester*. The former was a Cambridge friend, and seems not to have bothered with the London literary scene; he had matriculated at Weever's college, Queens', in 1591, took his BA in 1594–5, became a Fellow of Corpus in 1597 and Master of Corpus in 1626. Middleton, however, had connections in London that operated as a literary pressure-group. Two other friends praised *The Legend of Humphrey*, Robert Allott and Michael Drayton; in the same year Allott brought out *England's Parnassus*, an anthology of 'the choicest flowers of our modern poet's where, as we shall see (p. 28), Drayton notched up more entries than any poet except Spenser, and both Middleton and Weever could be well pleased with the number of extracts from their few books. Weever, we should recall, had addressed an epigram to Michael Drayton, hailing him as the successor to Sir Philip Sidney, wit's mirror (i.23), and a joint epigram 'Ad Ro. Allott, & Chr. Middleton' (iv.4)—'Quick are your wits, sharp your conceits,/ Short, and more sweet, your lays.' The 'M. D.' who commended *Faunus and Melliflora* as a 'sweet melodious ditty', and described Weever as 'now in the budding of his youthful days', is generally thought to be Michael Drayton,[3] and much later, in *Funeral Monuments*, Weever quoted frequently from Drayton, referring to him as 'my fore remembered friend' (p. 510). In 1599 Weever may have been more closely acquainted with Allott, whose first book was published in that year (*Wit's Theater of the Little World*, a collection of prose extracts), and with Middleton, the author of *The historie of heauen* (verse, 1596) and of *The famous historie of Chinon of England* (prose, 1597). Allott had also written short commendatory poems for other men's books, including Nicholas Ling's *Politeuphuia* (1597), a work again praised by Drayton (in the second edition of 1598). And, we may note in passing, Middleton's *Chinon* was dedicated to 'Master Edward Stanley', as was Weever's *Faunus*: even though the *Chinon* dedication came from the printer, these were the only books ever dedicated to Edward Stanley,[4] another sign that Middleton and Weever were probably in touch.

Robert Allott remains something of a mystery. 'No biographical facts have come down about Allott', said the *Dictionary of National Biography*. '[Brydges] surmised that he was the Robert Allott who held a fellowship at St John's College, Cambridge, in 1599. There was also a publisher of this name in the early part of the seventeenth century; but we have no means of identifying the editor of *England's Parnassus* with either.' As Weever addressed other Fellows of St John's in flattering verses, and knew a number of students at this college (cf. p. 13), whilst the publisher only began to be active a quarter of a century later, I think it reasonable to assume that Allott was the Cambridge man. He had matriculated as a sizar from St John's *c*. 1592, took his BA in 1595–6, his MA in 1599, and later became

Linacre lecturer and, according to Venn, 'a celebrated physician'. Venn also recorded that a Christopher Middleton matriculated as a sizar from St John's in 1587, took his 'B.A. *circa* 1600; B.D. 1619'. Allott and Middleton could have been bracketed together by Weever, like Meriton and Mountain, because they belonged to the same college (*Epigrammes*, iv.4,19).

The stationer Nicholas Ling, who owned several bookshops in London between 1580 and 1607, must have been an important 'focal point' for the group. He was publisher or co-publisher of nine of Drayton's early books, and of two of Allott's, one of Middleton's and one of Weever's (*An Agnus Dei*, 1601). According to Drayton's biographer, Ling 'was himself an assiduous compiler and editor. He had a chief share with John Bodenham and Robert Allott in getting together material for such collections as *Wit's Commonwealth* (1597), *Politeuph[u]ia: Wit's Theater* (1599), *Bel-vedere* (1600), *England's Parnassus*, and ... *England's Helicon* (1600)'.[5] Although Ling first sponsored one of Weever's books in 1601, we observe the ex-student from Cambridge closing in on the publisher from 1599, through his friends. Ling, incidentally, had been apprenticed to Henry Bynneman, like Valentine Simmes (who printed all of Weever's early signed books); and Ling and Simmes 'had frequent business dealings later'.[6] The literary group to which Weever attached himself could be extremely useful—all the more so since it was heavily involved in anthologies, and consequently could 'puff' a struggling author's reputation.

From Weever's point of view, Valentine Simmes was probably even more important than Ling. Simmes not only printed the *Epigrammes*, *Faunus*, *The Mirror of Martyrs* and *An Agnus Dei* (all, incidentally, without benefit of entry in the Stationers' Register); he also published *Faunus*, and could have been the co-publisher of one or more of Weever's other works. Just one or two copies survive of the first editions of three of Weever's four early signed books; had more copies come down to us, variant imprints might have indicated that Simmes was sometimes a co-publisher as well as printer. We know that he 'shared the printing of at least sixteen books';[7] shared publishing was also quite common. To pursue this point briefly, the book of Weever's *Epigrammes* was printed 'by V. S. for Thomas Bushell, and are to be sold at his shop at the great north door of Paul's'. The shop was Bushell's, but only one copy of the *Epigrammes* survives with its title-page, so it is possible that this was a joint venture, and that other copies carried Simmes's name. Bushell, a bookseller from 1599 to 1617, had served his apprenticeship with Simmes's friend, Nicholas Ling, from 1591 to February 1599, and is only known to have been connected with one other book in 1599, T. M.'s *Micro-cynicon* ('six snarling satires'). Both were dangerous books in the year when satires were banned by the bishops; perhaps, then, Simmes used Bushell's name to screen his own.

Either as printer, or as printer and publisher, Valentine Simmes played a significant part in Weever's early career in London. We are fortunate in being able to make use of W. Craig Ferguson's monograph,[8] a valuable study of a most interesting man, which, as we shall see, provides the 'background' for several Weever mysteries. Here we learn that Simmes began his apprenticeship in the Stationers' Company in 1577, and received his freedom in 1585. In 1589 he was hired to print some of the 'Marprelate' tracts, virulent criticisms of the Church of England (and, therefore, of the government); his secret press was discovered, he was interrogated by the Privy Council, and probably tortured—the first of his many brushes with authority. In 1595 he printed another man's book, and was punished by the Stationers' Company; then, in the next few years, 'came a number of small infractions ... He was one of the fourteen printers warned by the Company upon receipt of the commandments from Archbishop Whitgift and Bishop Bancroft on June 1, 1599. In October he had some "printed papers Remaynning in hall", and the Master and Wardens are to deal with him about it.'[9]

Whitgift's decree of June 1599 was, I think, more serious for Simmes and Weever than Ferguson indicated. Whitgift and Bancroft were in charge of book censorship at this time, and they now banned a large number of books that were either scurrilously satiric or erotic, which were publicly burned on 4 June 1599, in 'the bishops' bonfire'. They also ordered 'that no satires or epigrammes be printed hereafter'. Since Weever's *Epigrammes* were dedicated to Sir Richard Hoghton, who was knighted in June 1599, Simmes and Weever flouted the bishops' decree not long after it was issued, before it became clear that the authorities would not apply the new rules too rigorously. (Had they been questioned, Simmes and Weever might have pretended that the *Epigrammes* were printed before June; we know, however, that this could not be true.) A year later, when Simmes printed and published Weever's second book, *Faunus and Melliflora*, the risk of punishment would not seem so great, even though Weever here combined erotic and satiric interests. In the same year Simmes published other books that disregarded the decree—satirical works by Nicholas Breton, and Tourneur's *The Transformed Metamorphosis*. Why did he take such a gamble? Ferguson has shown that there was a dramatic fall in the amount of typesetting done in Simmes's shop in the years 1597–1602, from 8,500 metres in 1596 to between 2,000 and 3,000 metres a year in 1597–1602, rising again steeply in 1603–5.[10] The years in which Simmes printed Weever's poetry and other banned books were lean years, when he may have had to accept whatever work came his way, and even to take risks with satirical books that might have led to fines or imprisonment.

An undated letter in the Hatfield Papers, of around 1607, alleged that Simmes had made a habit of printing forbidden books. 'Valentine Symmes, who was now taken printing seditious books, has done the like seven times before this; first he printed the things of Martin Marprelate, after he has been meddling in Popish books, [and] he by forbearing has become worse.'[11] Since he had printed both Puritan and Catholic books, we may infer that Simmes was impelled by his purse, not his conscience. He needed the work: and that probably explains why he printed Weever's first two publications, which also fell into the category of forbidden books. They were not his most dangerous infringements, but more law-abiding printers would not have touched them.

Is it conceivable that Simmes was also responsible for *The Whipping of the Satyre* (1601), an anonymous book of satirical verse and prose that has been assigned, on internal grounds, to John Weever (cf. p. 37)? Ferguson observed that Simmes used a false imprint in 1598, giving Simon Stafford's name instead of his own.[12] In the revised *Short-Title Catalogue* of English printed books (1475–1640), we find that 'Quires B,D,F, [of *The Whipping*] have paper with horizontal chainlines', and that the imprint is '[S. Stafford] for J. Flasket'. Somewhat oddly, in Weever's *Mirror of Martyrs*, printed by Simmes in 1601, 'quires B,D,F have horizontal chainlines' (*ibid.*); I drew Professor Ferguson's attention to this coincidence, and he assured me (privately) that *The Whipping* 'was indeed set by Stafford ... I would assign the book to Stafford on the basis of the types used.' I do not dispute his conclusion, but I wonder whether Simmes, an ingenious lawbreaker if ever there was one, who had used Stafford's name as a 'screen' before, who had printed all four of Weever's signed books of verse and seems to have been the stationer most active in promoting his work, could have been in some way connected with *The Whipping of the Satyre*.

Simmes is best known today as the printer of some of the most famous plays of Shakespeare—*Richard II* (1597), *Richard III* (1597), *Much Ado* (1600), *Henry IV*, Part 2 (1600), *Hamlet* (1603)—as also of reprints of some of these first editions. Moreover, he printed other plays that are still read (at least, by students): Chapman's *An Humorous Days Mirth* (1599) and *The Gentleman Usher* (1606), Dekker's *The Shoemaker's Holiday* (1600) and *The Honest Whore* (1604), Marlowe's *Dr Faustus* (1604) and Marston's *The Malcontent* (1604), to name just a few. It is easy to forget that these admired plays were not immediately seen as gilt-edged securities by the stationers: plays and poetry were thought of as ephemera in the trade, not to be confused with weightier works, such as bibles or lawbooks. Simmes printed and published whatever came to hand—a play by Shakespeare, a satire by Weever—and may not have been as conscious as we are that some poets are better than others.

While Ling and Simmes were probably the stationers who most actively promoted the work of John Weever and his literary associates, a third stationer must not be forgotten. Allotts' *England's Parnassus* (1600) was published by Ling, Cuthbert Burbie and Thomas Hayes; and Burbie had also published Christopher Middleton's *The famous historie of Chinon of*

England (1597). Between these two dates came another joint venture, Nashe's *Lenten stuffe* (1599), printed by T. Judson and V. Simmes for N. Ling and C. Burbie. One of the most respected figures in the Stationers' Company, Burbie had also published the second in a series of books apparently inspired by Ling: (1) *Politeuphuia, or Wit's Commonwealth* (1597), compiled and published by Ling; (2) Francis Meres, *Palladis Tamia: Wit's Treasury, being the second part of Wit's Commonwealth* (1598), published by C. Burbie; and (3) Robert Allott's *Wit's Theater of the little world* (1599), published by Ling. (In the quotation from Newdigate, cited above on p. 23, *Politeuph[u]ia* is wrongly identified with *Wit's Theater*.) Burbie, as is well known, was also the publisher of two of Shakespeare's 'good quartos': *Love's Labour's Lost* (1598), 'Newly corrected and augmented', and *Romeo and Juliet* (1599), 'Newly corrected, augmented, and amended'. *Romeo and Juliet* replaced an earlier unauthorised or 'bad' quarto, and, though no earlier quarto of *Love's Labour's Lost* now survives, it is usually assumed that, in this case too, Burbie's edition replaced an inferior one. The players, it seems, finding that stolen and surreptitious versions of two of their plays had got into print, decided to issue better texts which they gave to Burbie—'whom', said A. W. Pollard, 'we must regard as the first of their confidential publishers'.[13] The 'copyright' of the two plays was thus acquired by Burbie and, incidentally, was later (in 1607) transferred by him to Nicholas Ling.

Burbie's connection with Ling is more important than has been realised because these two stationers and their associates played a crucial role in publicising the work of William Shakespeare. Not one of Shakespeare's plays had been issued with his name on the title-page before 1598; in 1598 twelve plays were identified as his in Meres's *Palladis Tamia* (published by Burbie) and, for the first time, three plays carried his name on the title-page—the second quarto of *Richard II* (printed by V. Simmes for A. Wise); the second quarto of *Richard III* (printed by T. Creede for A. Wise); and the first surviving quarto of *Love's Labour's Lost*, published by Burbie. The exact date of publication of the three plays in 1598 is not known, but it is noteworthy that Burbie published Meres's *Palladis Tamia* (with a dedication dated 19 October 1598), where twelve plays were first assigned to Shakespeare, and *Love's Labour's Lost* with Shakespeare's name, and almost certainly also acted as the confidential agent of Shakespeare's company. Burbie could have given Meres the list of Shakespeare's plays, or Meres's list could have drawn Burbie's attention to the fact that it would help to sell *Love's Labour's Lost* if the dramatist's name were attached.

Just before *Palladis Tamia*, Burbie had also published Meres's translation of *Granado's devotion* (by Luis of Granada; S. R. 28 March 1598). So Meres, a Cambridge graduate who was living in London in 1597 or earlier,[14] and who had a quite exceptional knowledge of the London literary scene and its gossip, was probably a member of the Ling—Burbie group. This is confirmed by his use of Ling's subtitle as the subtitle of *Palladis Tamia*, the second of the 'Wit' compilations; and, more decisively, by Meres's remark that 'Michael Drayton is now in penning in English verse a poem called *Polu-olbion* geographical and hydrographical of all the forests, woods, mountains, fountains, rivers, lakes, floods, baths and springs that be in England.' As Newdigate observed, Meres must have heard of this project 'from Drayton himself, for the First Part of the great undertaking was not to see the light till fourteen years later'.[15] And here let us recall that Meres also knew about Shakespeare's private penning—his 'sugared sonnets among his private friends'.

Meres and Drayton were evidently good friends. Michael Drayton, said Meres (p. 281b), 'quem toties honoris & amoris causa nomino' (whom I name so often on account of the esteem and love [I bear him]), is a man 'of virtuous disposition, honest conversation, and well governed carriage'. Although there is no positive evidence that Weever and Meres were personally acquainted, these two Cambridge graduates were members of the same 'pressure-group'; and that group, which may not have included Shakespeare but was certainly close to him, cannot be described as backward in promoting the interests of the various writers and stationers who belonged to it. McKerrow said of Weever's *Epigrammes* that, 'with the exception of the *Palladis Tamia* of Francis Meres, there is, I think, no single work of so early a date which contains references by name to so many Elizabethan writers of the first or second rank'.[16] McKerrow seems to have thought this a matter of chance; I believe, on the contrary, that it may have been because they belonged to the same group—one that adopted new methods of publicising contemporary writers, and in particular other members of their own group.

This survey of Weever's literary friends and connections at the turn of the century must now go back to *England's Parnassus*, the anthology of poetical extracts compiled by Robert Allott and published by Nicholas Ling (together with C. Burby and T. Hayes) in 1600. An invaluable edition of this anthology by Charles Crawford (Oxford, 1913) tracked down most of the 2,349 extracts to their sources (Allott merely assigned all but sixty-eight to an author, not always correctly). According to Crawford, the thirteen extracts from John Weever could not be traced, but must have been 'copied from an unknown work by the poet, written in or after 1598, seeing that in several cases it can be shown that the extracts are manifest borrowings from the 1598 edition of Sidney's *Arcadia*, and the *Hero and Leander* of Marlowe, issued in the same year'.[17] All of these 'untraced' quotations come, it was later pointed out, from *Faunus and Melliflora* (1600); we cannot blame Crawford for failing to notice this—the only surviving copy of *Faunus*, now in the Huntington Library, was probably not available for inspection in 1913. It is surprising, though, that when Arnold Davenport edited *Faunus* (in 1948) he overlooked the existence of

England's Parnassus, and failed to inform the reader that Weever's second book impressed the anthologist in the very year in which it was published. This was all the more regrettable since Crawford had identified the 'sources' of many passages in *Faunus* that were left unannotated by Davenport (principally borrowings from the *Arcadia*).[18]

Allott printed 13 extracts from Weever, as compared with 386 from Spenser (the front runner), 225 from Drayton, 171 from Warner, 140 from both Daniel and Harington, 123 from Sylvester, 119 from Lodge, and 95 from Shakespeare. (If these look like strange ratings to us, especially the figure for Warner, it may be relevant that Spenser, Drayton, Warner, Daniel and Shakespeare had all been praised in Weever's *Epigrammes*.) Weever's score is a respectable one, considering the figures for some other also-rans: Marston 17, Jonson 14, King James of Scotland 11, Guilpin 7, Sir Thomas Wyatt 6, the Earl of Surrey 1. We must not take these figures too seriously; on the other hand, Crawford's warning that Allott favoured his friends probably went too far in the other direction.

> Allott, apparently, was not the man to overlook friends, for he seems to have been only too eager to find places in his book for them, no matter what kind of rubbish they wrote, as witness the case of the poetaster John Weever, who is cited thirteen times. In the previous year, 1599, Weever praised Allott and Christopher Middleton in one of his *Epigrams*; hence the friend of the compiler is favoured, notwithstanding the fact that he was a wretched poet, who stole from others what we find commendable in him, and marred much of that.[19]

Having succeeded in tracing so many of Weever's 'sources', Crawford was over-inclined to convict him of thieving, quite ignoring the fact that such borrowing was normal at this time; and, knowing only Weever's extracts, and not their context in *Faunus*, he was critically unsighted, as it were, and in no position to judge whether Weever 'marred' what he borrowed or changed it for good reasons. Crawford's prejudice against Weever is evident in his comment on a 21-line extract describing Venus:

> Now in ire
> She mounts her chariot, swifter than the wind
> Or subtle comprehension of the mind,
> Which by two nimble cock-sparrows was drawn
> Caparisoned but lightly with the lawn
> Took from the flower-de-luce's inner skin,
> Trapped and embossed with marigolds: within
> Sits Venus naked, holding in her hand
> A tumbling shellfish ...

Crawford noted that this passage 'reminds one very much of *Romeo and Juliet*, I.iv.55; and it seems to be too good to be by Weever'.[20] Yet we now know that it was by Weever: it comes, again, from *Faunus* (ll. 1627 ff.).

That Weever and Allott were friends cannot be denied; and literary friends do sometimes praise each other, and probably expect to be repaid in kind. It is relevant that Weever bracketed together the names of Robert Allott and Christopher Middleton in a flattering epigram (iv.4), and that in the following year, as already stated, both Weever and Allott contributed complimentary verses to Middleton's *The Legend of Humphrey Duke of Glocester* (1600), while Allott quoted thirteen extracts from Weever and twenty-four from Middleton in *England's Parnassus*. It looks like literary back-scratching. At the same time it is strange that Allott totally disregarded the *Epigrammes*, where Weever had praised him, and concentrated instead on *Faunus*. I conclude, for better or worse, that Allott selected what appealed to him: he thought well of Weever (partly, perhaps, because Weever had praised him), but his was not a blind allegiance. He preferred Weever's non-satirical verse, and may well have wished to steer his friend in this other direction; Weever, however, judged differently, for in 1601 he indulged himself by writing *The Whipping of the Satyre*.

Before we leave *England's Parnassus*, one other point must be raised. Many of Allott's extracts contain 'variant readings'; Crawford argued that 'only in a few cases are his variants worthy of note and of adoption', since Allott can be proved to have been careless as a copyist. At the same time he showed that Allott, in a few instances, 'renders authors differently from all texts of their works that are extant, and in a manner which convincingly shows that such authors must almost certainly have allowed him to have access to their manuscripts'.[21] There are variant readings in some of the passages quoted in *England's Parnassus* from *Faunus*; as Weever seems to have been Allott's friend, some of these variants could derive from a manuscript; or, as only one copy of *Faunus* has come down to us, it is also possible that Allott preserved the readings of another copy, either corrected or uncorrected. The lines in *Faunus* that echo Weever's epigram on Shakespeare may illustrate:

> And thus faire words and power attractiue beuty,
> Bring men to women in subjectiue duety.
> (*Faunus*, ll. 295–6)
> ... Faire words and powre-attractiue bewtie,
> Bring men to want on in subiectiue dutie.
> (*England's Parnassus*, no. 102)

'To wanton in subjective duty' makes excellent sense in the context ('Thus Faunus swallowed Cupid's golden hook', l. 290 ff.), and, I think, is an instance where we should 'prefer the harder reading'.

Having described the literary circle which welcomed Weever in London—Allott, Middleton, Drayton, Ling and Simmes—I must now add that at least two other circles were aware of Weever but treated him less kindly. There are clear signs (explored in Chapter V) that he wished to break into the theatrical world; the epigrams he addressed to Edward Alleyn, Shakespeare and Jonson, and his many other allusions in the *Epi-*

grammes to theatrical affairs (cf. p. 18), can leave us in little doubt about this. Also, he saw himself as a satirist, praised and censured fellow satirists—Hall, Marston, Jonson, Guilpin—and perhaps regarded himself as one of the leaders of this new literary movement. Three of his five early books are wholly or largely satirical; satirists, however, are not noted for their camaraderie, and they did not overwhelm young John Weever with their congratulations. In fact, not one of his three satirical books caused enough of a stir to call for a second edition; Weever must have concluded that his genius as a satirist was not properly appreciated.

So much for the literary scene. Next, the date of composition of Weever's early works, which is less straightforward than at first appears. The *Epigrammes* must have been written over a period of years, more or less completed in 1598, and finally published in the second half of 1599. I discuss the evidence in detail in a separate section (p. 87 ff.), and turn at once to Weever's second book, *Faunus and Melliflora* (1600), a strange miscellany that seems to have been very hurriedly thrown together. Here is Arnold Davenport's account of its contents and their genesis:

> This book begins as an erotic poem in the line of *Hero and Leander* and *Venus and Adonis*. Until we reach line 1029 there is no sign that it is to be anything else. Then it suddenly turns into a mythological account of the origin of Satires; translations of the Latin satirists are dragged in with very thin excuse; and the story is briefly concluded with a few lines about the ecclesiastical ban on satires in 1599 and the burning of satirical books. Then follows an ironic satire disguised as 'A Prophecie' in which, following Joseph Hall's example, ... Weever pretends to rebuke satirists for attacking the present age, which is quite free from vice.[22]

Davenport argued that this odd 'mixture of kinds and styles' could be explained on the hypothesis that Weever, in June 1599, had two unfinished works in preparation, 'one an erotic poem very nearly completed, and the other a collection of fragments towards a book of satires translated and original'. On 1 June 1599, Weever's literary plans were threatened when the Bishop of London and Archbishop of Canterbury ordered the Stationers' Company to print no more satires or epigrams, and to call in and burn certain satirical and erotic publications. It is quite credible, said Davenport, 'that Weever should have attempted to evade the ban by cobbling together his two works in such a way that the erotic poem might pass as a mythological account of the origin of satire, and the satires themselves be presented as a deprecation of satire'.

Davenport's hypothesis plausibly accounts for the peculiarities of *Faunus and Melliflora* but, I think, fails to explain the full extent of Weever's dilemma after the ecclesiastical ban on satirical and erotic publications of 1 June 1599. This ban must have alarmed Weever even more than Davenport suggested because, apart from the two unfinished poems that were thrown together as *Faunus and Melliflora*, two other works from his pen probably awaited publication at the same time—the *Epigrammes*, and *The Mirror of Martyrs* (which, wrote Weever in 1601, 'some two years ago was made fit for the print').

Faunus and Melliflora concludes with 'A Prophecy of this present year, 1600', a poem intended for New Year's Day (l. 62). We may infer that this poem was written towards the end of 1599, and that the 'two unfinished works' included in *Faunus* were then in progress. The *Epigrammes* came out in the second half of 1599, and *The Mirror of Martyrs*, according to its author, belonged to the same year. Having invested a greal deal of time in the writing of poetry, therefore, Weever faced the possibility, in the autumn and winter of this year, that not one of his four books would see the light of day. Then he came across Valentine Simmes, 'one of the "untrustworthy" printers who were individually warned by the Stationers about the new orders' of 1 June,[23] and who, nevertheless, being short of work, was willing to take a risk. That explains, I think, why the young author's book was so shoddily printed (cf. p. 89); when Simmes at last found that he had nothing better to do and called for copy, Weever was not given the time to tidy his manuscript (he inserted the dedication to Sir Richard Hoghton, the newly knighted High Sheriff of Lancashire, but failed to upgrade the recipient of epigrams vi.1 and vii.16, 'Ad Richardum Houghton Militem'; and he did not manage to rearrange his *Epigrammes* in seven equal sections or 'weeks', as he seems to have intended). A little later, when Simmes offered to print another work by Weever, the same thing happened. The printer was in a hurry, the struggling young poet realised that it was a case of now or never—therefore he broke off (or rewrote) the ending of the poem 'Faunus and Melliflora', so as to give himself a half-excuse for tagging on his translations from Horace, Persius, and other satirical odds and ends. It made up another book, though not one that Weever had planned to write. His consciousness that *Faunus and Melliflora* was not a work to be proud of is visible, I think, in the note he inserted after a fragment translated from Juvenal: the author 'makes a vow that Juvenal, Horace and Persius shall hereafter all be translated'. He still saw himself as, potentially, a major literary figure, but he had suffered many frustrations.

My account of *Faunus and Melliflora*, not very different from Davenport's, fails to explain one perplexing fact. If Weever was so anxious to produce a second book that he could bring himself to jumble together totally unrelated poems, as described above, why did he not choose a less disreputable course—namely to publish *The Mirror of Martyrs* which, he later claimed, was already completed? The answer may be that no publisher wanted this poem on 'the life and death of that thrice valiant Captain, and most godly Martyr, Sir John Oldcastle'; at any rate, Weever implied that he himself kept the manuscript, not that a publisher accepted it and then refused to go ahead: 'This poem ... some two years ago was made fit for the print; that so long keeping the corner of my study, wherein I use to put waste paper, this first true Oldcastle thought himself injured, because he might not be suffered to sustain the second martyrdom of the press.' It could even be that Weever meant to hint that the printing of his poem was actually forbidden ('might not be suffered'), perhaps because the 'Oldcastle' story had already caused so much trouble; if this was the case, the performance and publication of Part One of the play, *Sir John Oldcastle* (by Munday, Drayton and others) could have cleared the way for Weever's poem.

Charles Crawford asserted long ago that *The Mirror of Martyrs* 'really had no existence prior to 1600, despite what the author says. *The Mirror of Martyrs* is literally packed from beginning to end with oddments stolen from Fairfax's *Godfrey of Bulloigne*, which was unknown before 1600'.[24] What, then, was Weever's motive for his statement about the poem's date? Poets do not usually brag about their inability to get their work published, so we want to know why Weever stressed this point. The reference to his poem as 'this first true Oldcastle' is suggestive: the Oldcastle play, as we happen to know from Henslowe's *Diary*, was first performed in November 1599; rightly or wrongly, Weever claimed that his poem preceded the play as the first 'true' *Oldcastle*. And, *pace* Crawford, Weever could have been right, since *Godfrey of Bulloigne* was entered in the Stationers' Register on 22 November 1599, and could have been entered a little after it was published, as sometimes happened, or even read by Weever in manuscript. It is not inconceivable that Weever was writing *The Mirror* in September–November 1599, before the Oldcastle play was performed, and felt that he could legitimately claim to have anticipated the play. It is an odd coincidence that two works, both presented as replies to Shakespeare's 'Oldcastle' plays, seem to have been written in the autumn of 1599, whereas Oldcastle had been replaced by Falstaff in *Henry IV* no later than 25 February 1598, when Part One was entered in the Stationers' Register 'with the conceited mirth of Sir John Falstaff'. That Weever and the *Oldcastle* dramatists should both have had the same idea two or more years too late, as it were, is unlikely; and, since one of the dramatists who collaborated on the play was Weever's friend Michael Drayton, I conclude that Weever wrote a version of his poem in 1599, could not get it published, spoke to Drayton about it, thus giving him the idea for the play, and perhaps expanded and completed his poem in 1601. Exactly when in 1601 the poem finally appeared in print we do not know, but, being dedicated to 'William Covell, Bachelor of Divinity', we may assume that it was before June, when Covell became a Doctor of Divinity.[25] Interestingly, the play (Part I of *Sir John Oldcastle*) was printed by Valentine Simmes; he perhaps agreed to print Weever's poem a year later because he found that, contrary to earlier expectations, there was a market for replies to Shakespeare's Falstaff plays. Be that as it may, we have no good reason to distrust

Weever's assertion that his poem 'was made fit for the print' two years before it was finally published.

Four of Weever's five early publications contain allusions to Shakespeare (the exception being *An Agnus Dei*). Apart from the implied rebuke in 'this first true Oldcastle', *The Mirror* also alludes to *Julius Caesar:*

> If thousands flock to hear a poet's pen
> To hear a god, how many millions then?

> The many-headed multitude were drawn
> By Brutus' speech that Caesar was ambitious.
> When eloquent Mark Antony had shown
> His virtues, who but Brutus then was vicious?
> Man's memory with new forgets the old,
> One tale is good until another's told.

Julius Caesar was first acted in 1599; Weever's tribute, that thousands flock to see it, would have been a very early one if these lines were also written in 1599.

If not Drayton's play, what gave Weever the idea to write in defence of 'that thrice valiant captain and most godly martyr, Sir John Oldcastle, Knight, Lord Cobham'? As Weever had gone out of his way to celebrate past and present members of his Cambridge college in *Epigrammes* (cf. p. 12), it may be significant that William Brooke, Lord Cobham, the Lord Chamberlain from August 1596 until his death on 5 March 1597, had been a student at Queens' College in his youth:[26] he and his son Henry Brooke, the next Lord Cobham, were direct descendants of the wife of the Lollard 'martyr' (Sir John Oldcastle, known as Lord Cobham after his marriage, was not an ancestor of the Elizabethan Cobhams), and Weever may have written his poem in the hope that this, together with the college connection, would win him an influential patron. Unluckily, the new Lord Cobham was not interested in supporting writers;[27] since he would be the obvious dedicatee for a defence of a former Lord Cobham, he may even have sent away the young poet unrewarded. In the end Weever dedicated his poem to his former tutor, William Covell, and a college interest is also visible in the verses addressed to his 'most honoured friend, Richard Dalton of Pilling' ('Rich. Dalton Lancast.' was admitted a Fellow Commoner at Queens' on 9 September 1595, and was also tutored by Covell). Perhaps Covell had pointed out the college connection, and, as a zealous religious reformer (cf. p. 17), had suggested that Sir John Oldcastle deserved more respect than Shakespeare had given him. Covell himself moved into 'Cobham territory' when he became vicar of Sittingbourne, Kent, in January 1603; and Weever must have toiled for years in the same territory, collecting inscriptions in the dioceses of Canterbury and Rochester (pp. 197–349 of *Funeral Monuments*). Later, however, Weever felt he had to repudiate Henry Brooke, Lord Cobham, who, 'stumbling upon a shallow-pated treason, which was laid in his way, fell down to the ground, together with his house, his inheritance, and all his additions of honour' (*Funeral Monuments*, p. 328; in his manuscript Weever expressed himself even more strongly: 'that unfortunate Lord Cobham ... involved in a foul, foolish + desperate design for the surprise of the king's person' in 1603).[28]

Although Weever's search for a patron is all too obvious at this time, his choice of a 'godly martyr' for his most ambitious poem so far had a secondary and equally transparent motive. As in his other acknowledged book of 1601, *An Agnus Dei*, Weever wished to signal to the world that he had religious interests and would respond to a call from the Church. (The fact that he had published 'low' satirical books, the *Epigrammes* and *Faunus and Melliflora*, would not disqualify him; others began as satirists and ended as clergymen—Stephen Gosson, John Donne, Joseph Hall, and John Marston.) The story of Sir John Oldcastle, which was told at length in Foxe's *Acts and Monuments* (1563), gave Weever opportunities to revile popish persecution and tyranny; Oldcastle, with whom the poet clearly sympathised, described himself

> As a true faith-professing Protestant,
> Not superstitious, nor too fond precise (D7b)

—in other words, a good Anglican! At the very end of the poem, when Oldcastle's ghost visits the poet and calls on him to tell his story, Weever takes the opportunity to present himself as a divine-in-waiting:

> Enter some watchful poet's secret mew,
> His heavenly thoughts, and quiet studies fright;
> With hollow voice commanding him set forth
> Immortal verse for my entombless worth. (F2a)

The 'heavenly thoughts' had not been too prominent in his satirical writing; a different image is now cultivated—hence, too, the dedication to Covell, a Bachelor of Divinity.

Yet, though we may detect these hopes behind the poem—a patron, or a career in the Church—it has to be said that *The Mirror of Martyrs* lacks a clear sense of literary purpose. The poem (244 six-line stanzas, rhyming ababcc) begins and ends as a tragedy told by Sir John himself, on the model of *The Mirror for Magistrates*, yet tries to be several other things as well. Every so often it slips into 'Spenserian' passages:

> Down in a dale enamelled with roses,
> Ten thousand Adons standing in a raw,
> And by a cranny which a garden closes,
> So many virgins and wood-nymphs I saw
>   With breasts half-hid, with loose-dishevelled hair,
>   To catch the balm-sweet breathing of the air
>
> Which gamesomely into their bosoms got,
> Whisks up and down, twines, curls up their tresses ...

A little later, Oldcastle's building of Rochester bridge once more triggers off Spenserian thoughts:

> Thus Medway, by this fair stone bridge adorned
> Made Thamesis enamoured of her beauty,
> All other rivers England had he scorned
> Yielding to her kind, love-deserving duty,
>   In smiles, embracements, gracious looks and greetings,
>   In amorous kisses, murmurs, night-set meetings.
>
> But how he courted, how himself he carried,
> And how the favour of this nymph he won,
> And with what pomp Thames was to Medway married,
> Sweet Spenser shows (O grief that Spenser's gone!) ... [29]

There are other digressions on dreams, comets, sodomites:

> Bewail may England sin of Sodomites,
> For idols and they are ground of all their woe,
> Of Simon Magus a sect of hypocrites
> Surnamed prelates are up with them to go
> And to uphold them in all that they may do.
>   You that be rulers peculiarly selected
>   How can you suffer such mischiefs uncorrected? (D3a)

The stanza that I have just quoted was lifted almost verbatim from John Bale's *Brief Chronicle concerning the examination and death of Sir John Oldcastle* (1544 etc.):[30]

> Bewayle maye Englande / the synne of Sodomytes.
> For Idolles and they / are grounde of all theyr wo.
> Of Simon Magus / a secte of hypocrytes
> Surnamed prelates / are vp with them to go.
> And to vpholde them / in all that they maye do.
> yow that be rewlers / peculyarlye selected.
> How can ye suffre / soche myscheues vncorrected?

This is a translation of a stanza in Latin ('Plangunt Anglorum Gentes crimen Sodomorum ... ') ascribed to Oldcastle, and also copied by Weever from Bale. 'For the latter part of Oldcastle's life Weever is indebted to Bale', explained L. M. Oliver, 'for he follows the latter's account closely, with many verbal echoes, and uses material from Bale's preface and conclusion that Foxe did not reprint'.[31] Bale was the source of some of Weever's errors—for example, making 'Reignold Cobham' Oldcastle's father.[32] A third book probably consulted by Weever is William Lambard's *Perambulation of Kent* (1576); like Lambard he devoted several pages to the building of Rochester bridge, though, unlike Lambard, he gave the chief credit for it to a Cobham. 'Of this [bridge] ... Sir Robert Knolles ... was the first author ... and of his own charge made over it the goodly work that now standeth ... At the east end of the same bridge, Sir John Cobham erected a chapel, and was not wanting to the principal work

itself'; Weever put it differently: 'Sir Robert Knowles was in the same an
actor / But Cobham was the chiefest benefactor'.[33] It is possible, however,
that Weever personally knew Rochester—as he certainly did later—and
wrote about the bridge from information obtained on the spot. Whatever
his sources, we may safely say that *The Mirror of Martyrs*—like *Faunus*
and *The Whipping of the Satyre*—tries to impress in too many loosely
related ways, and appears to have been written too quickly.

I have already indicated that Weever composed *The Mirror* in answer to
the Falstaff plays, claimed to have preceded Munday and Drayton's *Sir
John Oldcastle*, and was influenced by Spenser. Weever's poem also resembles Christopher Middleton's *The Legend of Humphrey Duke of
Glocester* (1600). Written in the same six-line stanza, both are long narra-
tive poems about the fall of a 'good' nobleman who resists the plots of a
prelate (Archbishop Arundel in Weever, Cardinal Beaufort in Middleton),
and who is finally hounded to his death. Both are patriotic and anti-
Catholic poems, and both are indirectly by-products of Shakespearian
plays. *The Legend of Humphrey* derives from *The Mirror for Magistrates*,
which had added 'Eleanor Cobham, Duchess of Gloucester' and 'Humphrey Plantagenet, Duke of Gloucester' to the edition of 1578, and from
Drayton's *England's heroicall epistles* (1597), but also includes a long
passage that seems to be indebted to *Henry VI, Part 2*. Shakespeare's
version of the tragedy of Good Duke Humphrey dramatised the farewell
of Duke Humphrey and his duchess when she leaves for the Isle of Man
with Sir John Stanley (II.4), and either a performance of Shakespeare's
play or the 'bad quarto' suggested a similar episode to Middleton. In the
play (II.4.82) and poem the Duke asks Stanley to 'use her well'; the duchess
chides, the duke recommends patience. While one expects these clichés in a
farewell-scene, Shakespeare had invented the scene, and made it mem-
orable. Middleton and Weever, it seems, both kept their eyes on Shakespeare;[34] and, since Duke Humphrey's duchess was a Cobham, perhaps
they both hoped to please the same patron—Henry Brooke Lord Cobham,
an important figure at Queen Elizabeth's court.

Weever's other signed work of 1601, *An Agnus Dei*, is in two senses a
smaller achievement; according to W. Craig Ferguson, this thumb book
'had the distinction of being the smallest book printed in England up to
that date'.[35] The revised *Short-Title Catalogue* describes it as '128°? in 8's';
it is so small (the page measures 37×30 mm and the actual type
26×22 mm) that some copies I have seen cannot be opened out or have lost
some letters next to the outer margin. The dedication of the first edition is
also cramped: 'To Her High Maiestie. Your humble Subject. Io: Weeuer.'
Three later editions are known, dated 1603, 1606 and 1610. After 1603
Weever changed the dedication to 'To Prince HENRY. Your humble servant *Io: Weeuer*', and added 'The Epistle Dedicatory': 'Thou matchless
issue of a mighty king, / To whose green years & judgment grave I bring /

These holy numbers of my heavenly muse, / Which my late empress deigned to peruse, … '. This tiny book must have been reprinted as a curiosity, not because of any intrinsic merit. Yet, though four editions are known, there are no copies in the British Library, the Bodleian, or Cambridge University Library (four of the surviving seven copies are in private hands), and so a description of the contents will be useful. Weever proceeds through the life of Jesus in sections that are often just two or four lines long, headed as follows: Mary's birth; her marriage; her salutation; conception; her visitation; Christ's nativity; man's ingratitude; his circumcision; the epiphany; the shepherds' vision; the flight into Egypt; Christ's return; the presentation; his childhood; Mary's search; his baptism; his travels; his miracles; his preaching; his feasting; his poverty; his piety; his humility; his love; his vertues; the Jews conspire; Christ's sweat; his betraying; Peter weepeth; Judas despairs; Christ arraigned; he was mocked; led to death; he prays; to the thief; woman, behold; thy son; my God; he thirsts; all ended; the wonders; the wounds; Christ's will and testament; his funerals; his resurrection; his ascension. The verse is uniformly pedestrian:

> In love he came the Nazarites to teach,
> And on a text of Esay he doth preach,
> Physician, heal thy self. Amongst thine own
> Who will accept thee? Art not Joseph's son?
> His own are angry, yet he scapes away,
> And in Capernaum taught the sabbath day, …

As far as I can see, there are no sinister doctrinal implications in this very condensed account of the life of Jesus. Only the book's title might surprise an orthodox Anglican, since 'Agnus Dei' could refer to the part of the mass beginning 'Agnus Dei … ', or to a cake of wax stamped with a figure and blessed by the Pope; Weever, however, no doubt composed it to prove himself an unexceptionable Anglican.

I have referred to Weever's third book of 1601, *The Whipping of the Satyre*, as 'unsigned', but this is not strictly true. The epistle 'To the vainglorious, the Satirist, Epigrammatist, and Humorist', and the following verses 'Ad Lectorem', are both signed 'W. I.', Weever's initials reversed. Arnold Davenport has shown that the author must be Weever, in whose acknowledged books there are several significant anticipations or echoes of *The Whipping*. The clinching one, I think, is the following:

> *In Nigellum.*
> If I should choose, yea, for my life,
> To be thy hawk, Nigel, or wife,
> I would the hawk choose of the one,
> She wears a hood, thy wife wears none.
>
> (*Epigrammes*, i.19)

A gentleman he was of right good blood
To whom I said, 'Faith, sir, you are to blame,
Beside your wife to keep one in a hood
For your own pleasure, whom I well could name.'
''Wounds, blood!' quoth he. 'Prove who, or thou shalt die!'
'Content yourself: it is your hawk', quoth I.
                                   (*The Whipping*, 457 ff.)

The gentleman is described a few lines earlier as 'a friend of mine' (*The Whipping*, 453), and, as I suggested in Chapter III, many of the joke-epigrams were addressed to identifiable friends or contemporaries of Weever at Cambridge. Both poems, I take it, allude to the same leg-pull.

Davenport also argued that Weever's three targets in *The Whipping* must be Marston (the satirist), Guilpin (the epigrammatist) and Jonson, and that Guilpin was the author of an anonymous reply, *The Whipper of the Satire his penance in a white sheet* (1601). We may add that both Jonson and Marston hit out at Weever and *The Whipping* in the very year when this satire was published (cf. pp. 47 and 44), which supports Davenport's identification of the 'whipper' and of his three opponents.

In *The Whipping* Weever adopted the same stanza as in *The Mirror of Martyrs*, rhyming ababcc. *The Whipping* also resembles *Faunus and Melliflora* in somewhat abruptly changing from 'The Pilgrim's Story' (ll. 1–156) to invective against the Satirist (ll. 157–618) and against the Epigrammatist and Humorist (ll. 619–1038), as *Faunus* had switched from an erotic romance to satirical verses. This time, however, the introductory pilgrim's story is more closely integrated with what follows, though the change of tone is equally noticeable. The narrator tells us that he was on a pilgrimage

              unto the holy town
    By which the waves of Jordan's crystal flood
    With silver surge quietly wanders down, (1–3)

when he chanced to spy 'two twin-like sisters', who 'discontented sit' lamenting the crosses they have to bear. It quickly transpires that they represent 'the sacred Church' and the 'Commonwealth' (135). Their crosses, says Commonwealth, are three men 'that viper-like would eat my bowels out':

    Sat., rough, severe; *Ep.*, skip-Jack jester-like;
    Hu., with newfangled neuterism enflamed,
    All naught.

The pilgrim steps forward, offers to bestow 'some pains' on the three villains, and the sisters promptly charge him with this congenial task.

Davenport noted the ingenuity of this introduction. *The Whipping*, being in the first place 'a deprecation of satire', could have been 'suggested by the ban placed on satires by the Licensers of the Press on 1 June, 1599'.

'"W. I.", the author, may have thought it a clever plan to write satirically about satire and satirists and so exploit the contemporary popularity of satire while at the same time appearing to support the Archbishop's objection to satires'.[36] I suspect, though, that the introduction also served another purpose. Weever, whose two other publications in 1601 intimate that he hoped for a career in the Church, depicts himself as a 'pilgrim' heading for the Holy Land, a man of God who stoops to satire from the highest motives—for the benefit of the Church and his country. First and foremost he still wants to be seen as a man dedicated to religion.

Turning now to the satirical stanzas, by far the longest part of the book, it is important to recognise that Marston receives his come-uppance first, and that Guilpin and Jonson are let off more lightly. The number of lines assigned to each of the three opponents is itself revealing, the more so when we observe that Weever slips into general invective against all three towards the end, around line 859: that means that he devotes 461 lines to Marston, then 240 to Guilpin and Jonson together, then 179 to all three. Marston comes out an easy winner, or loser. Why so?

Once more we are indebted to Arnold Davenport, whose posthumous edition of *The Poems of John Marston* (1961) completed a valuable series of studies of satirists at the turn of the century.

> In his *Epigrammes* ... Weever had attacked Hall and praised Marston. In *Faunus and Melliflora* he changes his ground. Though he ostensibly disapproves of satire, he now places *Virgidemiae* first and *The Scourge of Villanie* second; and his allusions in *A Prophecie* [in *Faunus*] to *The Scourge of Villanie* could not possibly have been relished by Marston. Indeed, the impression left by Weever now is that Marston knew about vices because he practised them.[37]

Exactly why Weever changed sides is not clear. One reason could be that he discovered that he had more in common with Hall's Puritanism than with Marston's brand of free-booting satire; also, Hall, a Fellow of Emmanuel College from 1595 and evidently heading for a career in the Church (he was ordained in December 1600),[38] might be useful in promoting Weever's clerical ambitions, whereas Marston did not behave like a future divine at this time, even if he later abandoned the theatre for the pulpit. The overriding reason, however, could have been Marston's quarrel with Jonson, which began in 1599 and continued in 1600 and 1601. As I suggest in Chapter V, Weever was lampooned in 1601 as an admiring hanger-on of Jonson; he may have thought of himself as coming to Jonson's rescue in *Faunus and Melliflora*, and harsh words could easily have followed during a personal encounter with Marston. At any rate, the attack on Marston in *The Whipping* was not a sudden about-turn but continued, with greater zest, Weever's previous detraction. What is surprising is not that Marston serves as the prize target in *The Whipping*, but that Jonson also receives a drubbing. The explanation of this may be that Jonson responded sarcastically to Weever's overtures, and that the stage-

portraits of Weever as Jonson's infatuated admirer were a cruel reminder
of a friendship that had already cooled (cf. p. 47).

Grappling with three quite formidable opponents, Weever wisely tried
to conceal his identity—a common precaution amongst satirists at this
time. Jonson probably guessed it, though, for he probably referred to *The
Whipping* in *Poetaster*, making Tucca say of Horace (i.e. Jonson himself):
'Fough! body of Jove! I'll have the slave whipped one of these days for his
satires and his humours, by one cashiered clerk or another' (IV.1). Dekker
also referred to *The Whipping* in *Satiromastix* a little later: 'I have laid
rods in piss and vinegar for thee. It shall not be the *Whipping a' the Satyre*,
nor the whipping of the blind bear, but of a counterfeit juggler that steals
the name of Horace' (V.2.243). The two plays are usually dated around the
middle of the year 1601,[39] yet *The Whipping* (S. R., 14 August 1601) must
have come out just before. Two more substantial replies to *The Whipping*
followed in the autumn of 1601: *No Whipping, nor tripping, but a kind
friendly snipping* (S. R., 16 September) and *The Whipper of the Satire his
penance in a white sheet* (S. R., 6 November). Davenport has shown that
the first was by Nicholas Breton, a prolific scribbler of verses, and the
second almost certainly by Edward Guilpin, one of Weever's three targets
in *The Whipping*.

That Jonson did not know the identity of the 'cashiered clerk' seems
unlikely. Dekker made Tucca threaten Jonson with something worse than
'the *Whipping a'th Satyre*' when Horace and Asinius Bubo (Jonson and
Weever) have just been 'untrussed' together, so Dekker also seems to have
known of Weever's authorship. Whether or not Guilpin knew that it was
Weever who had attacked him is uncertain; Breton addressed 'W. I.', as
'whosoe'er thou art', but also said of him 'I mean such striplings as perhaps he is' (*stripling*: one who is slender as a strip; one whose figure is not
yet filled out (*OED*)), and asks 'Or were you then at Cambridge?' He may
have had his suspicions as to Weever's authorship, affecting not to care:
'But what, where, when, or who, I care not'.[40]

A curious sequel to the publication of *The Whipping* came in 1604,
when an unknown scribe copied out the whole text in a poetical commonplace book, which is now in the Folger Shakespeare Library. This is a
beautifully written manuscript, and contains transcripts of other recent
publications, mostly satirical works dating from 1600 to 1604, and also
some apparently unpublished material. We cannot assume that the copyist
chose to write out these works because they were no longer available in
print, for the manuscript includes Drayton's *The Owl*, which went
through several editions in 1604 (S. R., 8 February) and must have been
easily available. Somewhat unusually, the scribe noted the day and month
when he completed each text, so we know that he copied *The Owl* between 10 and 21 April, and *The Whipping* between 29 April and 8 May.
There are a few minor variants in the manuscript—chiefly singulars/

plurals, and other small slips or corrections. In general, though, it is a remarkably faithful transcript, even following the printed version in some obvious misprints (e.g. 'Hk' for 'He', l. 465), therefore the presence of a small number of more significant variants could indicate that the copyist worked from a lost edition. (The epistle is signed 'Your friend. W. I.', not just 'W. I.'; some of the running titles read 'THE Whipping/of ye SATYRES' and this form of the title was used for the entry in the Stationers' Register (Arber, III, 190).)

The Folger commonplace book included Samuel Rowlands's *The letting of humours blood in the head-vaine* (1600), which was marginally concerned in the Poetomachia. *The Whipping of the Satyre* is the only work copied out by the anonymous scribe that could claim to have played a leading part in the war of the (satirical) poets and, rebuking both Jonson and Marston, in the War of the Theatres. Though it may not have been the last of Weever's early books to be published, *The Whipping* therefore gives us an interesting glimpse of his position in the literary world in 1601—a considerable advance in around four years. It places him close to the centre, whereas in the *Epigrammes* he had looked in from the outside. Others, predictably, questioned his right to such eminence, but, after several years on the fringe of the literary scene, he now saw himself as the equal of established poets and dramatists. Their response will emerge more fully in the next chapter: it only remains to be said that neither their lampoons of Weever nor his implicit claim to a leading role, as whipper of Jonson and Marston, should be taken too literally.

V

Satirical portraits of Weever in English plays, 1598–1601

Our picture of Weever in his early years in Cambridge and London could be that of any needy adventurer determined to make himself known in the literary world. There were many other young graduates who quickly produced two or three collections of poems or pamphlets, hoping that a wealthy patron would be pleased, and would thereafter provide for them. In addition, as we have seen (p. 18), Weever was interested in the theatre. I assume that he hoped to write plays; whether he did or not, other playwrights seem to have lampooned him as a familiar figure—not too surprisingly, since he himself participated vigorously in satirical mud-slinging and, as we shall see, was a very small man, therefore easily caricatured. Lampoons, of course, are slippery things; I must warn the reader that in this chapter we tread upon treacherous ground. If I am correct in my identifications, however, we also find Weever in excellent company, with Jonson, Marston, Dekker and Shakespeare.

(i) LONDON

Weever left clues as to his own personal appearance in *Funeral Monuments*, and they help to identify him (for the first time, I believe) as 'Asinius Bubo' in Dekker's *Satiromastix* (1601). This is a malicious portrait, but one that sharply differentiates him from the crowd of literary aspirants; with Bubo as our starting-point, we can then proceed to other lampoons in other plays.

Writing of William Drulege (p. 258), 'a man of stature like little *Zacheus*, but of a mind immense and vigorous', Weever could not resist adding that a 'little man is as much a man as the greatest man of the guard. But I may be thought quickly to speak somewhat partially, being none of those puissant pikemen: enough then of little men, if not a little too much.' And again, of John Baconthorp, 'the resolute little Doctor':

He was like another *Zacheus*, little of stature, but immense in wit and understanding, insomuch as it was a wonder to know so many virtues inhabit together in so small a mansion...For, if the bulk or pile of the books which he writ had been put into a bag, and laid upon his shoulders, questionless it would have pressed the slender short dwarf to death, saith my foresaid Author.

Much more might be said of this little-great man, but I am called for myself to the Press; and to speak more than I have done in the praise of little men, I may be thought to flatter myself. (p. 798)

(Compare *Luke* xix. 1–10: 'And, behold, there was a man named Zacchaeus ... And he sought to see Jesus who he was; and he could not ... because he was little of stature.') Weever, by his own admission, was a little man—considerably smaller than others, perhaps almost a dwarf. Now the smallness of Asinius Bubo is a constant subject for banter in *Satiromastix*, as in this exchange with Captain Tucca:

> *Asin.* Morrow, Captain Tucca, will you whiff this morning?
> *Tucca.* Art thou there, goat's pizzle? no, godamercy, Cain, I am for no whiffs, I; come hither, sheep-skin-weaver, s'foot thou look'st as though thou'dst begged out of a jail ... draw near: this way, march, follow your commander, you scoundrel.
>
> (I.2.292 ff.)

'Sheep-skin-weaver' is a nonce-word, and was clearly coined for a purpose. 'Goat's pizzle' is one of the less elegant allusions to Bubo's smallness; elsewhere he is described as a 'diminutive rogue', a 'small timber'd gentleman', Horace's [i.e. Jonson's] ape or beagle; and Tucca also calls him 'my little drum-stick', a 'slender gentleman' (Weever later compared himself with John Baconthorp, a 'slender short dwarf').

Bubo's 'commander', of course, is Horace [i.e. Ben Jonson]. Bubo breaks into raptures on hearing Horace's verses ('O pure, rich, there's heat in this', etc.), disperses Horace's epigrams amongst the gallants, and, encouraged by Horace, accepts a challenge from Captain Tucca: 'our credits', Horace tells him, 'lie pawn'd upon thy resolution', and Bubo squares up to the captain: 'Use me how you will; I am resolute, for I ha made my will.' (For the joke about Weever's *resolution* see p. 45.) Tucca climbs down ('so, I love thee, now I see th'art a little Hercules, and wilt fight'), and presumably we are meant to smile at the little man's triumph over a coward. In the play's final scene Horace and Bubo are 'pulled in by the horns, bound, both like satyrs', i.e. satirists; to escape further humiliation, Horace offers to have 'my satyr's coat pulled over mine ears', and Bubo echoes him—'And I too, let me be put to my shifts with mine ningle!' Both 'untruss' together, and this is the climax of *Satiromastix* (subtitled: 'Or, the untrussing of the Humorous Poet'). Since the play refers unequivocally to 'the *Whipping a 'th Satyre*' a few lines later, I deduce that Dekker believed Weever to be the author of this very recent publication—the only one of his works in which Weever posed, from first to last, as a satirist.

'Jonson is satirised as Horace', E. K. Chambers said long ago, writing of *Satiromastix*. 'Asinius Bubo is some unknown satellite of his, probably the same who appears as Simplicius Faber in Marston's *What You Will*.'[1] In Marston's play Jonson is represented as Lampatho Doria, and

> Simplicius Faber that Hermaphrodite
> *Party par pale*,[2] that bastard mongrel soul,
> Is nought but admiration and applause
> Of yon Lampatho Doria, a fusty cask ...
> Doth he [Lampatho] but speak, 'O tones of heaven itself!'
> Doth he once write, 'O Jesu, admirable!'
> Cries out Simplicius: then Lampatho spits
> And says, faith, 'tis good.[3]

What You Will (usually dated 1601, earlier in the year than *Satiromastix*) depicts Simplicius, in passing, as a smoker and a snob ('I'll have my ivory box of tobacco, I'll converse with none but counts and courtiers'), and, more insistently, as a lover of pretty boys: 'I am enamoured on thee, boy, wilt thou serve me?' Though himself short of cash, Simplicius seems to be less impoverished than Lampatho, and sometimes speaks as if Lampatho is his follower: 'What so, Lampatho, good truth I will not pay your ordinary if you come not.'[4] As his name indicates, he strikes others as a simpleton, a point repeated when he is dismissed in the last scene:

> The triple idiot's coxcomb crown thee,
> Bitter epigrams confound thee!
> Cuckold be whene'er thou bride thee.
> Through every comic scene be drawn,
> Never come thy clothes from pawn ...

For our purposes, though, the crucial thing is that Marston makes Simplicius a mindless adorer of Lampatho's [Jonson's] poetry, one whose rapturous exclamations resemble Bubo's in *Satiromastix*. 'Leave that staring fellow Admiration and Adoration', Simplicius is advised, 'a scorn on't, 'tis odious, too eager a defence argues a strong opposition.'[5] Here 'staring' perhaps makes the same point as the name Bubo ('owl'), that a small man's head seems disproportionately large, like an owl's, and that owls seem to stare.

'Through every comic scene be drawn' Marston had said derisively in *What You Will*. Could this be a hint that Weever had already figured in other plays? Bubo's first words to Captain Tucca, it will be remembered, are 'will you whiff this morning?' These are also his opening words elsewhere ('Demetrius Fannius, will you take a whiff this morning?'). Bubo's smoking is satirised by Dekker as an insufferable affectation—'I have always a consort of pipes about me' Bubo declares, and even his friend Horace finds it a bit much ('A pox a this tobacco!').[6] Now Bubo's characteristic word had already been used in *Every Man Out Of His Humour* as the nickname of Shift, 'a thread-bare shark' whose 'chief exercises are, taking the whiff, squiring a cockatrice, and making privy searches for imparters'; Shift is actually called 'Signior Whiff' in Jonson's play,[7] and the *Oxford English Dictionary* identifies this as the first known instance of *whiff*, sb.1, 2: 'an inhalation of tobacco-smoke; smoke so inhaled'. (Perhaps this nickname originated in a pun on the name Weever—whiffer?)

There are certainly other tobacco-enthusiasts in the plays of this period. The reason for identifying Shift, alias Signior Whiff, with the Weever caricatures in *What You Will* and *Satiromastix* is that, again, several significant jokes single out the same man. He is (1) an ostentatious tobacco-taker, (2) homosexual, (3) very small, (4) proud of his 'resolution', (5) exactly Weever's age. Here are some of the key passages, which drive me to the surprising conclusion that the man lampooned as Jonson's 'ningle' in *Satiromastix* was ridiculed by Jonson himself two years earlier, in *Every Man Out Of His Humour*.

(1) Shift puts up bills offering to teach young gentlemen 'to entertain the most gentleman-like use of tobacco; as first, to give it the most exquisite perfume; then, to know all the delicate sweet forms for the assumption of it; as also the rare corollary and practice of the Cuban ebolition, euripus and whiff', etc. A fool, Sogliardo, wishes to learn 'these sleights in tobacco', and Shift promises to 'bring him to the whiff' in a fortnight. Later others look through a keyhole to 'see Sogliardo sit in a chair, holding his snout up like a sow under an apple-tree, while the other [Shift] opened his nostrils with a poking-stick, to give the smoke a more free delivery'.[8]

(2) We are told of Sogliardo that 'his villainous Ganymede and he have been droning a tobacco-pipe ... ever since yesterday noon'.[9]

(3) In one of his bills, Shift describes himself as one 'who can serve in the nature of a gentleman-usher, and hath little legs of purpose'; Sogliardo is told that 'he [Shift] shall be your Judas, and you shall be his elder-tree to hang on'. Sogliardo asserts 'I think him [Shift] the tallest man living within the walls of Europe' (a double irony: *tallest* meaning bravest or biggest); and he persists with this word—'he is as ingenious a tall man as ever swaggered about London', etc.[10]

(4) Sogliardo and Shift engage in a tiresome game, addressing each other as Countenance and Resolution. This has clearly an extra-dramatic point, and is probably related to a similar sequence in *Satiromastix*, where Horace urges Bubo to show his resolution in fighting Tucca;[11] Shift, threatened, kneels to his adversary, much to Sogliardo's amazement; and, just as Tucca calls Bubo a 'little Hercules', Shift is addressed, ironically, as 'Hercules'.[12]

(5) In one of his bills Shift claims to be 'of the age of five or six and twenty at the most'. Weever was born in 1575 or 1576, therefore Shift's upper limit—not more than twenty-five or twenty-six—would be right for Weever in 1599.

The plays, it seems, have a single, identifiable individual as their target. How many men could there have been in London to fit this identikit? Only one, I would guess. Now we know that Weever paid his respects to Jonson in the *Epigrammes* and later criticised him, as well as Marston, in *The Whipping of the Satyre*; that is, Weever participated in the Poetomachia, and the three plays in which, as I have suggested, Weever was 'drawn through the comic scene', have always been recognised as skirmishes in that three-year war. In addition, Weever himself mentioned that he was a noticeably small man, and Tucca coined a very odd name for Bubo, that small-timbered gentleman—'sheep-skin-weaver'. Contemporary Londoners could have had little difficulty in recognising the victim of these various satirical attacks: he seems to have been a well-known 'character' in the literary-theatrical world at this time, like Marston and Jonson. (In the *Epigrammes* Weever paid his respects to Shakespeare and Edward Alleyn, leading members of the principal acting companies in London; we may deduce that he was trying to get a foothold in the theatrical world.) The wording of his dedications indicates that he was impecunious and needed financial support in 1599, exactly like Jonson's Shift, who 'searches for imparters' (i.e. bestowers, patrons): Weever addressed Sir Richard Hoghton as 'most bountiful Maecenas', and alluded to the generosity of other dedicatees, clearly with a view to lightening their purses.

Before we try to chart the ups and downs of Weever's relationship with Jonson we must look more closely at *The Whipping of the Satyre* which, as I have indicated (p. 40), came out in August 1601. Marston, rather than Jonson, is the principal target here, and the treatment of Jonson is revealingly ambivalent. Addressing Jonson in his epistle, Weever charged him with 'love of silver':

> you made sale of your Humours to the theatre, and there played pee-boh with the people in your humour, then out of your humour. I do not blame you for this: for though you were guilty of many other things, yet I dare say you were altogether without guilt [gilt] at that time ... I see you are one of those that, if a man can find in his purse to give him presently, they can find in their hearts to love him everlastingly ... I know but few but are corrivals with you in the love of silver ... And indeed I see no reason why every true subject should not love the queen's coin.

This is a tit-for-tat exercise, since Jonson had ridiculed Shift's 'privy searches for imparters', and had referred to a 'weaver of-phrases' whose begging was notorious and without rival (cf. p. 47). Yet, though Jonson was implicated in Weever's general remarks about the three satirists who deserved a whipping, Weever went out of his way to distinguish between Marston and 'the other two' (Guilpin and Jonson).

> Then let him take the other two apart
> And show how lewdly they their time misspent,

Who, being of a milder-moulded heart,
May happily in Christian sort relent.[13]

Later, having lashed Marston without much mercy, Weever again adopted a different tone for 'the other two':

Come hither now, friend Epigrammatist,
And do not wring my words to wrong my speech.
Hearken thou likewise, captious Humorist,
And hear that mildly what I friendly teach.
For those that speak in love and charity
Should both believèd and belovèd be.

While there can be no disputing the fact that Weever attacked Jonson in *The Whipping of the Satyre*, he did so more in sorrow than in anger. He showed his claws—understandably, for Jonson had not responded to his admiring overtures as he had hoped.

Let us list the principal events in their literary relationship, as far as we can reconstruct them. In 1599 Weever wrote flatteringly of Jonson and Marston in the *Epigrammes*, while Jonson ridiculed Weever as Shift or Signior Whiff in *Every Man Out Of His Humour*. A year later Weever attacked Marston (and therefore sided with Jonson) in *Faunus and Melliflora*. In 1601, when the War of the Theatres reached its climax, Weever treated Marston much more venomously than Jonson in *The Whipping of the Satyre*, and Dekker (in *Satiromastix*) and Marston (in *What You Will*) lampooned Weever as Jonson's hanger-on. (There would be a special sting in Dekker's and Marston's plays, of course, if Weever and Jonson had fallen out before they were caricatured: that is, if, after Weever had cooled in his admiration of Jonson, he were publicly reminded of it as a nauseating extravagance). Jonson, meanwhile, repaid Weever's attentions in an undated epigram:

To my mere English censurer.
To thee my way in epigrams seems new,
When both it is the old way, and the true.
Thou say'st, that cannot be, for thou hast seen
Davies and Weever, and the best have been,
And mine come nothing like. I hope so ... [14]

It is also possible that Jonson had Weever in mind in *Every Man In His Humour* (acted 1598, published 1601) when Lorenzo Junior marvels at Musco's clever impersonation of a decayed, ruinous, worm-eaten beggar, adding 'unless a man had juggled begging all his life-time, and been a weaver of phrases from his infancy for the apparelling of it, I think the world cannot produce his rival'.[15] If so, that would imply either that Weever was already known in London in 1598, or that Jonson inserted the dig about 'a weaver of phrases' in 1601. (Musco, incidentally, disguised as a begging soldier, describes his service in the wars, claims that he has 'nothing left me but my scars, the noted marks of *my resolution*', and offers to sell his worthless rapier. Is it a mere coincidence that in *Every Man Out Of His Humour* the impoverished Shift, 'that never was a soldier', nicknamed 'Resolution', is repeatedly asked whether he will sell his rapier, pretends to resent this affront and finally offers to sell it? Perhaps Jonson alluded in both plays to gossip circulating in London—viz., that Weever had been reduced to such straits that he had tried to sell his rapier.)

Whilst Weever's enthusiasm for Jonson gradually dwindled, Jonson seems never to have given him too much encouragement. We must remember, however, that the participants in the literary wars of 1598–1601 will have known each other personally, and that the surviving allusions in poems and plays are only a part of the story. Dekker and Marston—and, apparently, Shakespeare (cf. p. 50)—agreed in depicting Weever as Jonson's friend; Dekker, Marston and Shakespeare are known to have been Jonson's opponents in the War of the Theatres, and we need not regard their testimony as unimpeachable; on the other hand, since Weever made approaches to Jonson, and fiercely criticised Jonson's chief antagonist in the War of the Theatres, it is not easy to avoid the conclusion that Jonson and Weever were friends for a while. Jonson's published allusions to Weever may not strike us as friendly, but that in itself proves nothing: Jonson made far too many other scornful remarks about his known friends. As Drummond reported, he would rather 'lose a friend than a jest'.

How close was the friendship, while it lasted? In *Satiromastix* Bubo calls Horace 'my sweet ningle' at his first entrance, and Horace reciprocates with 'sweet rogue', 'honest rogue', 'good rogue' (all terms of endearment). Dekker hints that theirs is a homosexual friendship, a point also reinforced when Captain Tucca tells Horace 'Damn thee, thou thin-bearded Hermaphrodite', and also perhaps when Tucca asks Horace, 'Where's the syringe [i.e. Bubo] thou carriest about thee? O, have I found thee, my scouring-stick?'[16] Jonson's heterosexual preferences are well documented (for example, in his conversations with Drummond), so Dekker may slander both of his opponents. Yet *Every Man Out Of His Humour* and *What You Will*, as well as *Satiromastix*, both hint at Weever's homosexuality: it is therefore worth stressing that Weever wrote disapprovingly of 'soul-polluting sodomy' in several of his early books.

> O wakeful prophet that so far away
> Could spy the dawning of this New Year's Day,
> And in thy true authentic prophecy
> Foretell that brutish sensuality,
> Leopard-skinned, soul-polluting sodomy,
> Dog's appetite, and damned impiety
> Should be transported into Italy
> From England, this same year of Jubilee.[17]

(Compare *The Mirror of Martyrs*, D3a: 'Bewail may England sin of

Sodomites ...', quoted above, p. 35, and the *Epigrammes*, v. 14). At a time
when the accusations of satirists were quickly flung back at them by their
opponents it would be idiotic for a known homosexual to condemn
sodomy in a signed work; there was quite enough gratuitous mud-slinging
already. I conclude that Weever owed his reputation to malicious gossip,
which caught on, perhaps, because of his other colourful eccentricities. An
advocate of that filthy weed, tobacco, and a pushing poet—the more he
drew attention to himself the more likely it was that, sooner or later, the
little man would be slapped down; and since little John Weever tried to
attach himself to powerful friends, is it so surprising that those who dis-
liked him mocked him as a 'villainous Ganymede'?

The three 'anti-Weever' plays also agree in presenting him as a
tobacconist—can this be proved from other sources? Yes, it can: Weever
contributed two complimentary poems to Henry Buttes's *Dyet's Dry
Dinner* (1599), a collection that included Buttes's poem in praise of tobacco. In one of these poems Weever made it quite clear that he too was a
tobacco enthusiast:

> Diet's dry dinner? Change thy dinner's name,
> For, witty Buttes, thou doest thy dinner wrong.
> Of fish, fruit, flesh and white-meat dost thou frame
> A diet, with tobacco leaves among.
> And canst thou say thy dinner then is dry
> When both of spices and of sauces store
> And of tobacco's moisture fresh supply
> Thy dinner is replenished evermore?
> With salt of wit so sweet thy dinner seasoned
> And relished with the sharpness of thine art,
> The history of this thy diet reasoned,
> The table furnished rich in every part,
> > Change, change thy name: I see no reason why,
> > Buttes, thou shouldst call thy diet's dinner dry.

(ii) A DWARFISH ACTOR IN SHAKESPEARE'S COMPANY

The 'small timbered gentleman', Asinius Bubo, could only have been included in *Satiromastix* if Dekker knew that a dwarfish actor was available
to play the part for the Lord Chamberlain's Men. There are signs in other
plays that such an actor existed, and was a talented comedian. In *The
London Prodigal* (performed by the King's Men, according to the 1605
title-page) he appeared as Tom Civet, a ridiculous suitor, and was described in the following exchange:

Lance. O, I remember, a little man.
Art. Ay, a very little man.

> *Lance.* And yet a proper man.
> *Art.* A very proper, very little man.   (II.1.134 ff.)

In *Volpone*, performed by the King's Men in 1605, Nano the dwarf was given a much larger role than his companions, the eunuch and hermaphrodite, and must have been created for the 'Bubo' actor, as, I think, was Shift in *Every Man Out Of His Humour*.

Thus at least four plays performed by Shakespeare's company allude to the smallness of an actor who, we may reasonably suppose, was one and the same man. And what of Shakespeare's own plays? I believe that there are grounds for assigning three very different parts to the same diminutive comedian: Thersites, Master Slender and, unexpectedly, Sir Andrew Aguecheek. All three are found in plays fairly close to *Satiromastix* in date,[18] and in all three cases the dwarfish actor is 'protected' by a bigger man, as in *Satiromastix*—a traditional comic partnership.

While the commentators have paid more attention to Thersites' ugliness, his smallness is also clearly implied. *Toad-stool* and *cob-loaf* in II.1 and *fragment* (V.1.7) make the same point about Thersites, whose partner in this play is Ajax. (Compare *OED*, cob, 7a: a small loaf of roundish form.) Most of the experts, of those who accept that there is topical allusion in *Troilus and Cressida*, 'argue that Jonson is portrayed in the figure of Ajax'.[19] If so, that could mean that Ajax's dwarfish and foul-mouthed acolyte, Thersites, again stands for the dwarfish satirist, John Weever. It is a strange coincidence, at any rate, that the railing Thersites (whose relationship with Ajax resembles Weever's with Jonson in 1601) is called 'vile owl' (II.1.87) at the very time when Weever apparently figured as Bubo (owl) in *Satiromastix*.[20]

Master Slender, in *The Merry Wives of Windsor*, 'hath but a little whey face ['wee-face' in the Folio text], with a little yellow beard ... but he is as tall a man of his hands as any is between this and his head' (I.4.19ff). A *little* face, a *little* beard, but a *tall* man of his hands? Slender could mean small as well as thin in the early seventeenth century (*OED*, slender, 4), and Slender's name is no less meaningful than Master Shallow's or Mistress Quickly's. The point would not have to be made more explicitly if a 'very little man' appeared on the stage, as in *The London Prodigal*. Shakespeare, however, seems to glance at it elsewhere, as when Slender is asked repeatedly whether he 'can love' Anne Page, which takes on more ludicrous implications if a very small man's physical disadvantages are also in question. 'Can you carry your good will to the maid?' 'You must speak possitable, if you can carry her your desires towards her?' (I.1.210 ff.). And Slender is undoubtedly related to Sir Andrew Aguecheek, 'a thin-faced knave' (V.1.198; cf. 'wafer-faced' Bubo, I.2)[21] whose hair 'hangs like flax on a distaff' (I.3.96). Traditionally Sir Andrew is played by a tall, thin actor, perhaps because of Sir Toby's remark that 'he's as tall a man as any's in Illyria' (I.3.18). The tradition of a tall Sir Andrew, however, cannot be traced back to Elizabethan times; we have seen that Shift, in *Every Man Out Of His Humour*, was described as 'the tallest man living within the walls of Europe' (cf. p. 45), the same joke is made about Master Slender—so it could be the same joke again in *Twelfth Night*. Fabian says of Sir Andrew, 'This is a dear manikin to you, Sir Toby', an odd statement if Sir Andrew is tall (*OED*, manikin, 1: a little man, a dwarf); Sir Toby's whimsy about Sir Andrew's hair, 'I hope to see a huswife take thee between her legs and spin it off' (I.3.96), also makes better sense if Sir Andrew was played by a dwarf. Sir Andrew, of course, is a 'ridiculous suitor' like Master Slender and Tom Civet in *The London Prodigal*.

Much of the comedy in *Twelfth Night* would be altered if Sir Andrew is metamorphosed from tall to small. The vanity of a dwarf who thinks 'I have the back-trick simply as strong as any man in Illyria' (I.3.115) is more ludicrous; Sir Toby, admiring 'the excellent constitution of thy leg', and urging Sir Andrew to caper 'higher' (I.3.114 ff.), acquires a tinge of cruelty, a foretaste of the play's later blend of sunshine and rain; and Viola's duel with Sir Andrew becomes even more grotesque if Sir Andrew is not only a coward but, in addition, a pigmy wielding a man-sized sword.

The mimic of John Weever in *Satiromastix* (and, perhaps, in *Troilus and Cressida*) was probably a hired man with Shakespeare's company over a period of years. He and his partner, I suggest, acted Bubo and Horace, Slender and Shallow, Thersites and Ajax, Sir Andrew and Sir Toby. Only Bubo and Thersites, I think, referred to Weever. The 'Bubo' actor specialised in cowards and fools, and that may explain why he was made to portray Weever as he did; we need not suppose that the two dramatic characters had much in common with Weever's own.

(iii) CAMBRIDGE

I now move on to another play performed at roughly the same time. McKerrow observed that Weever's epigram on Gullio (ii.21) is 'alluded to by the character Gullio in the *Return from Parnassus*', a university play performed at Cambridge in 1599, 1600 or 1601.

> I am very lately registered in the rolls of fame, in an epigram made by a Cambridge man, one Weever—fellow, I warrant him, else could he never have had such a quick sight into my virtues, howsoever I merit his praise: if I meet with him I will vouchsafe to give him condign thanks.[22]

The fool Gullio here addresses Ingenioso, a former Cambridge student who said of himself in the first of the three Parnassus plays, 'I after many years' study ... looking still when I should meet with some good Maecenas, that liberally would reward my deserts, ... fed so long upon hope till I had almost starved.'[23] In *The Return* Ingenioso reappears in Cambridge (Parnassus) and is asked 'How goes the world with you?' This is his reply, from his very first speech in the play:

> As for my state, I am not put to my *shifts*; for I want *shifts* of shirts, bands and all things else, yet I remain thrice humbly and most affectionately bound to the right honourable printing-house for my poor *shifts* of apparel.
> *Studioso.* But I pray thee, how hast thou fared since I saw thee last?
> *Ingenioso.* In faith, *I have been pasted to every post* in Paul's churchyard *cum gratia et privilegio*, and like Dick Pinner have put out new books of the maker.[24]

This exchange, which includes an echo from one of Nashe's pamphlets,[25] makes three points that I find intriguing in a Cambridge play that elsewhere refers to Weever: a quibble on 'shift' (repeated again later: 'Ingenioso, how dost thou mean to shift for thy living?')[26], pasting to every post in St Paul's, and the claim that Ingenioso has 'put out new books'. For in *Every Man Out Of His Humour* the impecunious 'Shift' sets up his bills in St Paul's, and, I suggested, represents John Weever, who had also arrived in London from Cambridge and was trying to make a living as a writer. (As J. B. Leishman has shown, the author(s) of *The Return* and its sequel knew and repeatedly imitated Jonson's plays, so an allusion to Jonson's Shift would not be surprising.) Later in *The Return* Gullio brags of his poetry, and Ingenioso sarcastically retorts that 'every John Dringle can make a book in the commendations of temperance, against the seven deadly sins, but that's a rare wit that can make something of nothing, that can make an epigram of a mouse and an epitaph on a monkey!'[27] Now Weever's *Epigrammes* contained many poems on trivial subjects (like most epigram-books), an unusual number of epitaphs, and an epigram that 'made something of nothing':[28]

> *Ad Quintum*
> Thou asked one thing of me which I denied,
> That one thing nothing was, then thou replied.
> If it was nothing which thou asked of me
> Then nothing, Quintus, I denied to thee.
>   Now yet for nothing, one thing, Quintus, know:
>   For nothing something, Quintus, thou dost owe.

According to Leishman, Ingenioso 'almost certainly' stands for Thomas Nashe.[29] Why so? Nearly all of the allusions to Nashe occur in the third Parnassus play, *The Second Part of the Return from Parnassus*, perhaps because, as Leishman observed, Nashe 'was almost certainly alive' when the first two Parnassus plays were written but died before the third one followed a year or so later. I think it possible, therefore, that the author or authors of these tantalisingly allusive Cambridge plays metamorphosed Ingenioso from Weever to Nashe, in *The Second Part of the Return*, after this other son of Cambridge died suddenly, at the early age of thirty-four.

For Nashe was one of the first English authors to ridicule the practice of dedicating books to patrons, specialising in the mock-dedication, whereas Ingenioso, in *The Return*, is an assiduous searcher for patrons, which surely suggests a different target:

> *Studioso*. What patron is that you speak of? Art thou travelling toward a Maecenas?
> *Ingenioso*. In faith, laying a snare to catch a dottrel ... What a rewarder he is of witty devices! But indeed, he is a mere man of straw, a great lump of drowsy earth.[30]

When he is interviewed by his first patron, Ingenioso launches into a long speech that reads like a dedication ('Pardon, sir, the presumption of a poor scholar ... '), and Patron then reads aloud an extract from 'the epistle dedicatory', and gives Ingenioso a reward of two groats. A friend mocks Ingenioso's patron-chasing—'fiddling thy pamphlets from door to door like a blind harper, for bread and cheese, presenting thy poems like old brooms to every farmer';[31] and Ingenioso later serves Gullio as his 'suppliant poet', promising that 'if I live, I will limn out your virtues in such rude colours as I have'.[32] This does not suggest Nashe, who had ridiculed 'suppliant' dedications for some years, but rather a patron-pleasing poet (Nashe was principally a prose-writer); and Weever probably outgunned all other poets at this time in the ancient art of begging. (As Jonson said of Musco (cf. p. 47), in begging 'the world cannot produce his rival'.) Had the author of the *Epigrammes* not managed to insert seven dedications in his little book, some of them addressed to mere esquires, or country gentlemen? In addition, though, he had included many ingratiating poems addressed to high and low (the Earls of Cumberland and Rutland, Lord Monteagle, down to esquires and soldiers), as well as a number of commemorative poems on recently-deceased members of well-to-do families (the Earl of Derby; the son of the Lord Keeper; Robert Shute, a judge), whose grateful relatives might reasonably be expected to 'impart'. If there was one son of Cambridge who excelled in laying snares to catch dottrels that man was John Weever; even if he were not referred to by name in *The Return* we should have to consider him seriously as the model for Ingenioso, the recent Cambridge student who spends so much of his time in 'travelling towards a Maecenas'.

Another reason for this identification is that Ingenioso is aggressively partisan about tobacco. I have a pamphlet here, he boasts, 'that none is privy unto but a pint of wine and a pipe of tobacco'. And again:

> Why, this is the life of a man, to command a quick rapier in a tavern, to blow two or three simple fellows out of a room with a valiant oath, to bestow more smoke on the world with the draught of a pipe of tobacco than proceeds from the chimney of a solitary hall![33]

Nashe was not seen by his contemporaries as a flaunting 'tobacconist'

whereas Weever, I have suggested, was given this very image (Signior
Whiff, etc.) in three other plays.

If Weever is indeed represented by Ingenioso in *The Return* we must not
expect as derisive an account of him as we are given in *Every Man Out Of
His Humour*, *What You Will* and *Satiromastix*. The Cambridge authors
invite us to laugh at the desperate tricks of Ingenioso and other poor
scholars who struggle to advance in a hostile world, but naturally enough
they side with Ingenioso and his friends and treat them sympathetically. If
the identification is accepted it adds another twist to Gullio's allusion to
Weever, already quoted (p. 51), 'One Weever ... *if I meet with him* I will
vouchsafe to give him condign thanks': the fool is actually addressing
'Weever' without being aware of it (rather like the Clown in *The Winter's
Tale* IV.3, talking to an unrecognised Autolycus). More important for our
purposes, Ingenioso's quickness in spotting Gullio's garbled quotations
from Shakespeare suggests that he may be an identifiable Shakespeare
enthusiast.

> *Gullio.* Pardon, fair lady, though sick-thoughted Gullio makes amain unto
> thee, and like a bold-faced suitor gins to woo thee.
> *Ingenioso.* We shall have nothing but pure Shakespeare, and shreds of poetry
> that he hath gathered at the theatres.
> *Gullio.* Pardon me, moy mittressa, ast am a gentleman, the moon in comparison
> of thy bright hue a mere slut, Antony's Cleopatra a black-browed milkmaid,
> Helen a dowdy.
> *Ingenioso.* Mark, *Romeo and Juliet*: O monstrous theft! ...
> *Gullio.* Thrice fairer than myself, thus I began,
> The gods' fair riches, sweet above compare,
> Stain to all nymphs, more lovely than a man,
> More white and red than doves and roses are! ...
> *Ingenioso.* Sweet Master Shakespeare![34]

Ingenioso ridicules Gullio's enthusiasm for Shakespeare, which has turned
the fool into an unconscious plagiarist, yet Ingenioso's 'Sweet Master
Shakespeare' is double-edged if this irony comes from Ingenioso-Weever,
a vociferous Shakespeare-praiser, the author of a sonnet beginning
'Honey-tongued Shakespeare ... ' as also of a recently-published poem
(*Faunus and Melliflora*) crammed with Shakespeare-echoes!

John Weever and his *Epigrammes* are certainly targets in *The Return
from Parnassus*. It is interesting that several of Weever's jokes in the *Epigrammes* are also found in *The Return* and its sequel (*The Return*, Part 2)
and that Ingenioso is described as 'that *little* Mercury' in the sequel.[35] I
conclude that Ingenioso stands for Weever in *The Return*, or for a representative witty student who is at times meant to remind us of Weever; and
that in *The Return*, Part 2, this witty student could be a composite portrait
of Nashe and Weever and other notorious sons of Cambridge.[36] While
Weever did not achieve a national reputation equal to Nashe's, his thinly-
disguised attacks on fellow-students, many of which have now been de-

coded for the first time, must have made him a sensation at Cambridge, and the Parnassus plays were written for Cambridge. But there is an even better reason for identifying Weever as Ingenioso if, as was recently suggested by F. L. Huntley,[37] *The Pilgrimage to Parnassus*, the first of the three Parnassus plays, was actually written by Weever. The Prologue of *The Return* refers to the author of *The Pilgrimage* in tantalisingly elusive language:

Prologue

Gentle—
Stagekeeper. How! 'gentle' say you, cringing parasite?
That scraping leg, that dopping [dipping] courtesy,
That fawning bow, those sycophant's smooth terms
Gainèd our stage much favour, did they not?
Surely it made our poet a staid [stayed?] man,
Kept his proud neck from baser lambskin wear,
Had like to have made him senior sophister:
He was fain to take his course by Germany
Ere he could get a silly poor degree.
He never since durst name a piece of cheese,
Though Cheshire seems to privilege his name.

As Huntley explained, the Weaver is the principal river in Cheshire, hence 'Cheshire seems to privilege his name'. To which we may add that Weever went out of his way to emphasise the importance of the river Weaver in *The Mirror of Martyrs*:

I will but wade near to this river's brink
And of her deepness make this shallow boast:
Her cooling water those dry countries drink,
So she makes fruitful all the western coast
That no less famous, no less fair a river
Than the fifth Avon, or third Ouse, is Weever.[38]

and, we may assume, he will have sung the praises of this fair and famous river at Cambridge as well. The author or authors of *The Return from Parnassus* do not prove beyond all possibility of doubt that Weever wrote *The Pilgrimage* but, considering all the other digs at him, the attribution seems plausible. And since *The Pilgrimage* was almost certainly composed for the Christmas festivities of 1598, it ties in with the suggestion (cf. p. 18) that Weever saw himself as a future playwright while at Cambridge. He remained in touch with Cambridge after his arrival in London (cf. p. 77): he could have sent the play back from London, having failed, apparently, to win recognition in the capital as he had hoped.

Let us now sum up the case for identifying Ingenioso in *The Return* with John Weever. 'A student of the Parnassus Plays', said Leishman, 'should be continually on the look-out for particular as well as for general satire':[39] there is a strong presumption that Ingenioso stands for an individual well known at Cambridge. If so, the author of *The Pilgrimage* would be a prime target in *The Return*, which was written by one or more Cambridge men who already ridiculed the author of *The Pilgrimage* in their prologue. Granted *The Return* includes several quotations from Nashe, as from many other authors—yet Weever is named, his epigram on Gullio is referred to unmistakably, and another epigram that 'made something of nothing' could also be a tribute to Weever. Ingenioso's much-emphasised search for patrons to whom he can dedicate his poems surely points to Weever (a poet) rather than Nashe (chiefly a prose-writer, who mocked 'suppliant' dedications); and his being a 'tobacconist' is also significant. Weever, again, was a known Shakespeare-supporter, whereas Nashe (a close friend of Shakespeare's deceased enemy, Robert Greene) was not. The quibble on 'shift', and the allusion to Ingenioso's having been 'pasted to every post in Paul's', though they make sense if applied to Nashe, are really more amusing if applied to Shift-Weever of *Every Man Out Of His Humour*. I realise that some of the evidence is circumstantial, in so far as I have inferred from the plays performed in London that Weever was a notorious 'tobacconist' and was lampooned as 'Shift'; all the other evidence, however, is based directly on Weever's *Epigrammes*, that neglected treasury of literary gossip and inside information. Weever, who must have been as conspicuous a 'character' in Cambridge as in London, who kept in touch with Cambridge and praised its leading men in *Funeral Monuments* no less than in his *Epigrammes*, seems the best candidate for the part of Ingenioso; and this identification, if correct, gives us a more plausible portrait of John Weever at the turn of the century than does Signior Whiff or Simplicius Faber or Asinius Bubo, even though some of the satire in *The Return* may be aimed at poor scholars in general, not just at one man.

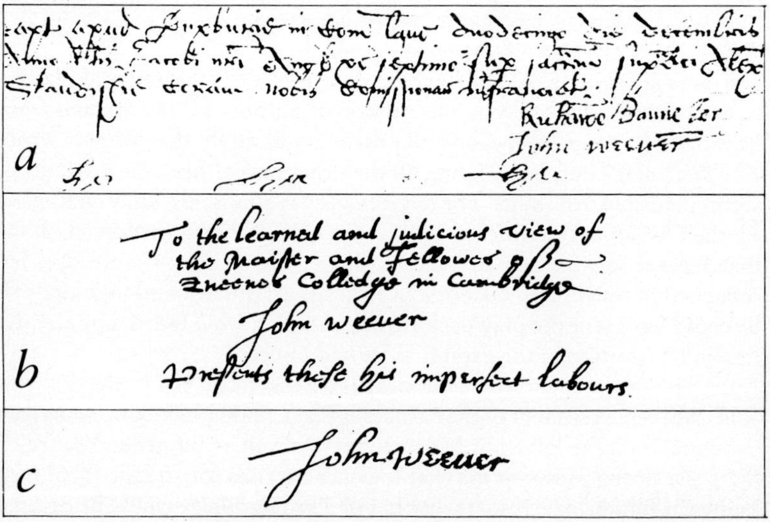

PLATE II   John Weever's signatures: (*a*) 1609, (*b*) 1631, (*c*) 1632, from his will

VI

From 1601 to 1631

◦⋙०⋘◦

How did Weever occupy himself between 1601, when he published his last books of poetry, and 1631, the date of *Funeral Monuments*? A silence of thirty years is so strange, considering the poet's bustling activity from 1599 to 1601, that W. T. Lowndes (cf. p. 3) evidently considered *Funeral Monuments* to be by a different author. Yet the antiquarian John Weever described himself as 'AEtatis Suae 55. Anno 1631', as a former student at Queens' College, Cambridge, a Lancastrian, a friend of Michael Drayton, so that we may say categorically that the poet and antiquarian were one and the same man. How, then, did Weever spend the years from 1601 to 1631? We have no information about his career, and it may be that, after impressing the London literary world as an impoverished hack, he found himself suddenly lifted to independence by a generous patron, and did not need a career. In his will he described himself as a 'gentleman', and named no trade or profession; he spent many years in collecting epitaphs, which suggests that he had independent means—and his house in Clerkenwell Close, which was still standing in the nineteenth century, gives the same impression. It was

> a large double-fronted house, faced with stucco; the rooms are spacious, and the ceilings of the best apartments are adorned with ornamental wreaths in plaster; the staircases are broad, and the balusters are massive. We should suppose from our own observation that the house was erected during the reign of the first James.[1]

The first item of 'worldly estate' in Weever's will also betokens a gentlemanly lifestyle: 'Item, I give and bequeath unto my brother William Weever my black cloak with many laces.'

Weever could have improved his lot by marrying a rich wife. If, however, he was very small, perhaps almost a dwarf (cf. p. 42), as well as an impecunious scholar, few ladies would have regarded him as a catch. I am therefore inclined to connect his later affluence with the tribute to Thomas Langton, the Baron of Newton and Baron of Walton—'my passionate affection to the dear memory of this party deceased (from whom I do acknowledge to have received many favours)'.[2] Langton came from a renowned family; when he died, 'with him the glory of that ancient race lies

buried'—or, to switch from Weever's words to those of a more modern
memorialist, at Langton's death without issue the barony of Newton
'went through an heir female—his aunt—to the family of Fleetwood'.[3]
Thomas Langton had inherited 'about 27,000 acres of land' and some 600
houses;[4] despite his later financial troubles (cf. p. 8), he could have provided for Weever's future, and may also have helped him in earlier years.
Let us recall Whittle's account of Weever: 'by the care of his uncle Thomas,
he was enabled to receive an excellent education', and he later enjoyed a
'small annuity'.[5] It is possible, as I have mentioned, that Thomas Langton
was Weever's uncle Thomas, or even that the poet was Langton's illegit-
imate son.

A Chancery suit of 1609 (*G. Blundell* v. *Sir Richard Hoghton, Alexander
Standish etc.*)[6] suggests that Weever may have owned property in
Lancashire at this date. 'John Weever' was one of the commissioners who
witnessed and signed depositions, and his signature closely resembles that
on the poet's will (Plate IIc). (Weever's other surviving signature, in the
copy of *Funeral Monuments* presented to Queens' College, differs slightly
in so far as he used a different 'e'; his tendency to switch from one 'e' to
another is visible in all of his manuscripts.) Only Justices of the Peace and
local men of some standing would normally serve as commissioners, so it
is possible that in 1609 Weever was a property-owner in Lancashire, not
merely a visitor. He could have inherited property from Sir Thomas
Langton, or from some other Lancashire relative or friend. Years later,
however, when he made his will, there was no suggestion that he possessed
property in Lancashire, whereas he disposed of the leases of two houses in
London. If he was a property-owner in Lancashire in 1609—and this is
only a conjecture—he could have sold out, and transferred his assets to
London, before 1632.

Exactly when he married is not known. One of the *Epigrammes* (i.22)
probably implies that he was unmarried when he wrote it, and it would be
strange if he was a married man when he published it, in 1599. He named
his wife, Anne Weever, in his will, and appears to have had no children.
This persuades me that Anne Weaver 'of the parish of St James, Clerkenwell', widow, who made her will in 1647, 'aged and weak in body but of
good and perfect mind', had been his wife. She has the right name, lived in
the same parish, was roughly the age to be expected, and also appears to
have had no children. Her reference to 'my brother Paul Onion' reveals her
maiden name, unless brother meant brother-in-law or half-brother, and
the Onion family may yet open doors for future students of Weever.
(Could the Onions have been connected with the theatre? Peter Onion, in
Jonson's *The Case Is Altered*, consorts with Antonio Balladino, the 'page-
ant poet' to the city, i.e. Anthony Munday; if the name Onion, like
Antonio, identified a known individual, it is interesting that the Onions of
East Grinstead were called 'Onion, alias Divell',[7] and that one of Peter

Onion's friends turns on him with 'avoid, Mephistophilus!' (II.4)). Anne Weaver, who bequeathed a feather-bed, table cloths and napkins in her will, and a table 'standing in the hall', seems to have belonged to the same socio-economic group as John Weever, a 'gentleman'. Although she referred to none of John Weever's relatives in her will, she fits in with the known facts so neatly that it is reasonable to conclude that the poet married a lady unromantically named Anne Onion.

Whatever the source of his funds, Weever was able to travel extensively in Great Britain and on the continent between 1601 and 1631. There are several hints of this in *Funeral Monuments*. He was at York in 1603:

> *Suavis victoria Amor populi*. The love of the people was a pleasant sweet conquest (a motto which I saw depicted under the arms of our late sovereign lord King James, over one of the gates of York, upon his first auspicious entrance into that ancient city, *Ann.* 1603, *die Aprilis* 16). (p. 358)

It may have been at the same time or a little later that Weever visited Kendal: 'They call this Corpus Christi Play in my country, which I have seen acted at Preston, and Lancaster, and last of all at Kendal, in the beginning of the reign of King James' (p. 405). He claimed, indeed, to have perambulated most of England and parts of Scotland, his ambition being 'to publish to the view of the world, as well the modern, as the ancient memorials of the dead throughout all his Majesty's ... dominions':

> With painful expenses ... I travelled over the most parts of all England, and some part of Scotland; I collected the funeral inscriptions of all the cathedral churches of the one, and in some of the other, and ever by the way gathered such as I found in parochial churches. ('To the Reader')

As for his travels overseas, there are some passing references in *Funeral Monuments*; for example, his note on Sir John Mandeville—'I am sure that within these few years I saw his tomb in the city of Liège' (p. 568). 'And who would not visit Rome, if abilities of body and means were all sufficient?' he asked elsewhere, marvelling at a city made honourable by ruins, as Montaigne had said, 'and as I myself, being there, did also observe' (p. 40). His unpublished manuscripts fill out the picture. Writing of English churches before the Reformation, he said that they were 'superstitiously painted, carved or insculped with the effigies, similitude or image of Christ ... as I have seen and read in the Roman Catholic churches of Italy, France and Germany'.[8] He then quoted verses from churches in Paris, Milan, Naples, etc., and, while it is possible that he copied some from other men's books, there are clear signs that he visited some or all of these places. The note on one epitaph, 'which I saw and copied out from a tomb in the church of a little town in France called Colleure',[9] is fuller than most; he usually named the church and town, without repeating that he was personally there, but we may take it that he 'saw and copied out' most of these verses. He may even have gone as far as Spain, though he did not

mention it in referring to Catholic countries he had visited. Francis Cotting-
ton wrote from Madrid in 1610 that an unidentified 'Mr Weaver is still in
Seville. I have written to him this day'.[10]

Travelling overseas, Weever could have been attached to the retinue of
an ambassador or nobleman. As a collector of antiquities at home, however, he seems to have acted on his own—hence his 'painful expenses' (cf.
p. 59)—over a period of many years. In the end he felt

> altogether discouraged to proceed any further in this my laborious and
> expenseful enterprise, until I came casually into the acquaintance of my dear
> deceased friend, Augustine Vincent, Esq., Windsor Herald, and Keeper of the
> Records in the Tower, who persuaded me to go forward as I had begun, and
> withal gave me many church collections, with divers memorable notes, and
> copies of records, gathered by himself and others; and by his means I had free
> access to the Heralds' Office.

Here, in his Epistle 'To the Reader', Weever implied that he had already
collected the inscriptions of all the cathedrals in England, and of some in
Scotland, as well as gathering antiquities elsewhere, *before* he met Augustine Vincent; for, as he said, '*after all this scrutiny* ... I was altogether
discouraged to proceed any further' (my italics). It is not possible to date
Weever's meeting with Vincent precisely,[11] although much of the material
in Weever's MS. 128 seems to have been transcribed from Vincent's MSS.,
or from records in Vincent's charge; on fo. 104b, Weever wrote 'here ends
the collections of Oxfordshire, lent unto me by my new friend A. Vincent',
and on fo. 253 (and again later) he noted 'out of the records in the Tower'.
These notes, again, cannot be dated exactly, but it seems probable that
Weever's friendship with Vincent ripened over four or five years before
Vincent died in January 1626, and that Weever had toiled for years on his
own before he met the Windsor Herald. I conclude that Weever must have
been actively involved in his 'laborious enterprise' in the second and third
decades of the century, and may well have begun shortly after he stopped
publishing poetry in 1601.

As he acknowledged, Weever's meeting with Augustine Vincent was
particularly important. The heralds were responsible for the funerals of all
armorial families, and kept elaborate notes on the funeral arrangements
for major figures; they were 'funeral specialists', and could advise Weever
when he needed help. Again, Weever's interest in funeral monuments often
involved him in family history, where the heralds or their records could
also offer guidance. And as Keeper of the Records in the Tower, Vincent
could help Weever financially. We know from other diligent searchers for
antiquities that they had to brace themselves for expenses over and above
the cost of travel. A. Agard, in *The Repertorie of Records* (1631), a 'brief
introductive index' to records at Westminster, etc., warns the reader about
fees: 'the search of anything' in the Tower, for example, 'is ten shillings' (p.
11). Vincent might have excused Weever from these dues—and perhaps

from others. 'By his means' wrote Weever (of Vincent), 'I had free access to the Heralds' Office, to write out such antiquities as I could there find for my purpose' ('To the Reader'). Vincent opened many doors for Weever who, surprisingly, seems to have worked in comparative isolation even though there were scholars in London who shared his antiquarian enthusiasms. 'Above all, I am most bound to love the foresaid Vincent's memory for that he made me known to that honourable gentleman, Sir Robert Cotton, ... [who] lent me out of his inestimable library such books and manuscripts as were most fitting for my use.' Cotton died just three weeks before Weever composed his epistle 'To the Reader', but many others had also helped: Sir Henry Spelman and John Selden, Esq., 'the most learned antiquaries now living of our times'; Sir Simonds D'Ewes; and 'divers of the heralds'—Sir Richard and Sir Henry St George, John Philipot, William Le Neve and others.

Since Augustine Vincent became Weever's closest friend and helper in his antiquarian labours, I must pause to give a brief account of his career (partly based on the *Dictionary of National Biography*).[12] Born around 1584, Vincent was appointed Rouge Rose pursuivant extraordinary in 1616, Rouge Croix pursuivant in 1621, and Windsor Herald in June 1624. A friend of William Camden, who made him his deputy to visit Northamptonshire and Rutland in 1618, he supported Camden (1551–1623) in his bitter quarrel with Ralph Brooke, the York Herald. Camden had been appointed Clarenceux King-at-arms in 1597; Brooke published his criticism of Camden's accuracy in 1599, Camden replied, Brooke replied, and the College of Arms remained for many years divided between the two factions. Brooke returned to the attack in *A Catalogue* (1619), and Vincent answered for the other side in *A discoverie of errours* (1622), printed, as Brooke's *Catalogue* had been, by William Jaggard. Vincent's book is well known, for he allowed Jaggard space to defend himself against Brooke's charge that he, the printer, had introduced errors into Brooke's *Catalogue*—and Jaggard, who naturally thought well of the workmanship in his own printing-house, was at this very time busy with Shakespeare's First Folio. We may assume that Vincent, like Weever, was an admirer of Shakespeare: he owned a presentation copy of the First Folio, in which he recorded that he received it from Jaggard 'anno 1623'.

Vincent is unlikely to have given Weever 'free access to the Heralds' Office' before 1616. I think, indeed, that the two men must have met for the first time after 1621, perhaps as late as 1623 or 1624. That they were acquainted by 1624 is established by a note, 'Out of a paper book borrowed of Mr Vincent of the pedigrees of Littleton, Quatermayne, Burghley ... A[nn]o d[omin]i 1624';[13] and, as Vincent was so closely connected with Camden, it is probably significant that Weever did not claim to know Camden when he listed the Clarenceux Kings-at-arms, but said of Camden's successor, Sir Richard St George, that he was 'a gentleman ever

ready to give me his best furtherance in this work' (*Funeral Monuments*,
673–4). Camden, however, was ill in his last years, and that may explain
why Weever apparently did not receive help from him.

Although Vincent published only one book he was an industrious writer
on heraldry and antiquities, and his manuscripts form a valuable collection. Most of them are in the library of the College of Arms, which is
shortly to issue a catalogue that identifies Vincent's own compositions and
those of some of his friends (not including Weever). The late Windsor
Herald, 'my dear deceased friend', was evidently a kindred spirit, who
shared Weever's enthusiasms. He was not merely a collector of antiquities:
one has only to read through the chapter-headings of Vincent MS. 87 in the
College of Arms (*Parentalia, or, Funeral Rites, Ceremonies, and Solemn-
ities ... according to the antique and modern customs of sundry nations
and times*) to discover how much he had in common with the
historical-philosophical approach of Weever's eighteen introductory
chapters:

> 1. Of man's being, his fall, and his repair ... 2. Sickness an intermedium between
> life and death ... 3. Divers sorts of death ... 4. Offices of piety done to the
> deceasing and after they are deceased. Sugillation what. Stretching forth of the
> limbs ... 5. Removing the corpse into the hall ... 6. Of mourning and mourners
> ... 13. The time of production of the dead among the Grecians ... 14. Divers
> sorts of funerals among the Romans.

Before the chance meeting with Vincent, Weever worked on his own for
many years. This is surprising, as I have said, at a time when antiquarian
studies already attracted considerable interest. Robert Cotton, Weever's
later friend, began to collect his books and manuscripts around 1588;
shortly before Queen Elizabeth's death in 1603, Cotton and others petit-
ioned the Queen to set up an Academy for the study of Antiquity and
History, stating that 'there are divers gentlemen studious of this knowledge and which have of a long time assembled and exercised themselves
therein'.[14] They referred to the first Society of Antiquaries, which began to
hold meetings in London about 1586 and continued until about 1608, with
discourses or papers on agreed topics. Sometimes the discourses made up a
series; early in 1600 there were several on funerals and funeral customs.
The members of the Society 'were many of them knights and all of them
gentlemen except their honoured colleague John Stow; many of them
owned manorial rights and were interested in the conditions of the tenure
of land in England'.[15] When formal meetings ceased, the Heralds' Office
and Robert Cotton's library continued to bring antiquaries together, yet
Weever, until fairly well advanced with his work, seems not to have had
the entrée to either.

It should not be forgotten, however, that Michael Drayton, another
poet keen on antiquarian study and Weever's friend, was already intimate

with Stow and Camden in the 1590s, as B. H. Newdigate has shown (*Michael Drayton*, p. 92 ff.). Perhaps, then, Weever had contact with sympathetic antiquarian friends and Augustine Vincent was merely the first one who actively helped him.

Apart from the general interest in all things antiquarian, which flourished in London—where Weever lived from 1598 to 1601, at the end of his life, and probably during most of the intervening period—there was a European interest in 'funeral monuments' that was also firmly established. In his epistle 'To the Reader' Weever mentioned the books of 'Schraderus, Chytraeus, Swertius, and other foreign writers'. English authors did not lag far behind—witness Camden's *Reges, reginae, nobiles et alii in ecclesia collegiata B. Petri Westmonasterii sepulti* (1600) and H. Holland's *Monumenta sepulchraria Sancti Pauli* (1614). Weever's most important English predecessor was probably John Stow, whose *Survey of London* (1598 etc.) included many epitaphs in English. Sometimes Weever may have reprinted verses from Stow (compare Stow, ed. 1618, p. 450 ff. and Weever, p. 405 ff.), but in general he avoided repeating Stow's material, which was easily available. Stow's later editors, Anthony Munday and H. Dyson, added many epitaphs after 1598, it should be noted, including John Weever's one year after he died.

Although *Funeral Monuments* is a folio of almost 900 pages, it may be asked whether the author really needed thirty years for it when Camden and other antiquaries achieved much more in less time. Here we have to remember that while Weever dealt with only four dioceses in the folio (Canterbury, Rochester, London, and Norwich), he had completed most of his collections for the rest of England and for parts of Scotland: the book he published represented only a fraction of the work he had done. At one stage he may have intended at least one more volume for the other English dioceses (witness a manuscript note on 'the ancient and honourable name of the Gerards, of whom hereafter in my second part');[16] when he prepared *Funeral Monuments* for the press, however, he decided to exclude epitaphs of 'later times' and only to print 'those of more antiquity' ('To the Reader'), explaining that those 'of later times ... I reserve for another volume' (p. 314). It seems, then, that he had at least two more volumes 'in active preparation', and this helps to account for the years from 1601 to 1631. In addition it is relevant that, although he received some help from friends, especially in his later years, most of his sources were neither printed books nor manuscripts but 'monuments' scattered throughout the country which he personally inspected, travelling on horseback; and also that, over and above his successful visits, he made many trips that ended in disappointment.

> Having found one or two ancient funeral inscriptions ... in this or that parish church, I have ridden to ten parish churches distant from that, and not found

one. Besides I have been taken up in divers churches by the churchwardens of the parish, and not suffered to write the epitaphs ... for that I wanted a commission ('To the Reader').

Weever could not plan his trips methodically, as would now be possible, because he lacked reliable information as to where to go, not to mention public transport. He depended on hearsay; if an unusual monument was unearthed, as happened in 1630 while he was preparing his book for the press, there were no newspapers to draw attention to it. But there was public interest; the discovery of a 'goodly' monument, together with a coffin and 'an ashy dry carcase' in a sheet of lead, was talked about—'to see all which, great confluence of people resorted, amongst which number I was not the hindmost' (p. 778). Considering his difficulties, and the fact that he must have retraced his steps in some parts of the country at various times, he achieved quite as much as other antiquarians who worked from books and manuscripts and did not travel as extensively.

While it seems perfectly possible that Weever dedicated his last thirty years to his passion for funeral monuments, without following any other career, it would be wrong to think of his life as consisting of two unrelated parts—the poet succeeded by the antiquarian. In his first book, the *Epigrammes*, his special interest in funeral verses is already visible: eighteen of the poems included are either epitaphs, 'jocose epitaphs', or deal with tombs. (Near the end of MS. 127 Weever added several pages headed 'jocose epitaphs', some in Latin, some in English; though his last book was more solemn than his first, his sense of fun, and delight in incongruity, remained with him for life.) Equally important, he did not give up the writing of poetry after 1601, even if he published no more under his own name. In *Funeral Monuments*, where poetry is often quoted (cf. p. 71), Weever almost always indicated its author's name—and the translator's, if the original was not in English—together with the source of his extract. Sometimes, however, he simply assigned his quotation to an unnamed writer, and some of these verses, especially when Weever described them as 'late' (i.e. recent), have long puzzled me—for one naturally wonders whether they might be his own. (Cf. p. 4, 'upon this forgotten city a nameless late writer hath made this epitaph'; p. 156, 'thus not long since Englished'; p. 492, 'one lately ... made these rimes following'.) There can be no doubt that many of the unassigned translations are by Weever, particularly when a short epitaph is followed without comment by an English version (e.g. p. 442), or when the original was copied from a monument, not from a book (p. 205). And it is significant that in his manuscripts Weever laid no claim to verses that he himself must have written (they are heavily corrected, and survive in a first draft and fair copy), for this confirms that unassigned verses in *Funeral Monuments* may be his as well. Here is an example (on Sir Thomas Gerard, Baron Gerard of Gerard's Bromley):

He died the 7 of October, 1617. Upon whom this epitaph was made.
    look over the leaf
        [he that in wars an army could command]
        [He that in peace could in obedience keep]
        [blank line]
        Now countermanded by imperious death
        lies buried in this vault here underneath.

Weever deleted the first two lines, left the next blank, and then tried again 'over the leaf':

He whose [high] undaunted spirit [durst] did out-face his foe
The horridst shape of foe by sea or land
He that his county ruled with awful grace
He that knew well an army to command,
    Now countermanded, ruled, out-faced by death
    Thomas Lord Gerard here lies underneath.[17]— —

One poem of unidentified authorship printed in *Funeral Monuments* (pp. 492–3) remains a mystery. It was tentatively assigned to W. Basse in *The Oxford Book of Seventeenth Century Verse* (1934, pp. 240–2), but was reprinted from Weever's volume. I think it possible that Weever was the poem's author, even though it is more impressive than most of his signed work; as I have pointed out elsewhere,[18] it resembles Weever's epitaph for Robert Shute (*Epigrammes*, iv.15) and, if his, might be so successful because written later than the poems of 1599–1601, by a more mature poet. I did not know, however, when I accepted Weever's authorship, that the poem was already in print before 1631. Let us begin with Weever's version.

One lately having taken view of the sepulchres of so many kings, nobles, and other eminent persons interred in this abbey of Westminster, made these rhymes following, which he called

A Memento for Mortality.
Mortality, behold and fear:
What a change of flesh is here!
Think how many royal bones
Sleep within this heap of stones,
Hence removed from beds of ease,   5
Dainty fare, and what might please,
Fretted roofs and costly shows,
To a roof that flats the nose,
Which proclaims all flesh is grass,
How the world's fair glories pass,   10
That there is not trust in health,
In youth, in age, in greatness, wealth.
For, if such could have reprieved,
Those had been immortal lived.
Know from this the world's a snare,   15
How that greatness is but care,
How all pleasures are but pain,

And how short they do remain.
For here they lie had realms and lands
That now want strength to stir their hands,   20
Where from their pulpits, sealed with dust,
They preach 'in greatness is no trust'.
Here's an acre sown indeed
With the richest royal seed
That the earth did e'er suck in   25
Since the first man died for sin.
Here the bones of birth have cried,
Though gods they were, as men have died.
Here are sands (ignoble things)
Dropped from the ruined sides of kings,   30
With whom the poor man's earth being shown
The difference is not easily known.
Here's a world of pomp and state,
Forgotten, dead, disconsolate.
Think then this scythe that mows down Kings,   35
Exempts no meaner mortal things.
Then bid the wanton lady tread
Amid the mazes of the dead,
And these truly understood
More shall cool and quench the blood   40
Than her many sports a day
And her nightly wanton play.
Bid her paint till day of doom
To this favour she must come.
Bid the merchant gather wealth,   45
The usurer exact by stealth,
The proud man beat it from his thought—
Yet to this shape all must be brought.

This poem must be later than *Hamlet*, being influenced by V.1.185 ff.; and, incidentally, it partly agrees with the first and partly with the second quarto of the play.[19] It first appeared in print in a collection sometimes ascribed to William Basse, *A Help to Discourse, or, A Miscellany of Merriment* ('consisting of witty, philosophical and astronomical questions and answers. As also, of epigrams, epitaphs, riddles and jests'), by 'W. B. and E. P.', which was issued at least seven times between 1619 and 1628. In *A Help to Discourse* we read:

A memento for mortality.
Taken from the view of Sepulchres of so many Kings and Nobles, as lie interred in the Abbey of Westminster.

and the poem follows, as in Weever, with very minor variants ('World', l.15; 'royalst', l.24; 'as men they dyde', l.28, in ed. 1619; 'worlds', l.15, in ed. 1621 etc.). Weever did not reprint Basse's sequel to *A memento*, 'A short addition or memento hereunto annexed upon the death of Queen Anne' (she died in 1619), but inserted in *Funeral Monuments* (p. 4) at least one other poem previously printed in *A Help to Discourse* (beginning 'Stay thy foot that passest by'). Although the earlier volume was called a 'miscellany', and drew on the work of many writers—could, therefore, have included an unpublished poem by Weever, who, we now know, went on composing funeral verses until 1617 or later—the authorship of *A Memento* is best described as 'uncertain'. We may say, however, that this interesting poem reflects Weever's taste, whether or not he himself wrote it.

The thirty years from 1601 to 1631 were not spent in idleness. Weever travelled at home and abroad, he continued to write poetry, and he may have continued with his projected translations of Juvenal, Horace and Persius (cf. 31); above all, he collected inscriptions from funeral monuments, many more than have reached us in the surviving manuscripts. The Folio of 1631 brought to notice only a fraction of the work already accomplished.

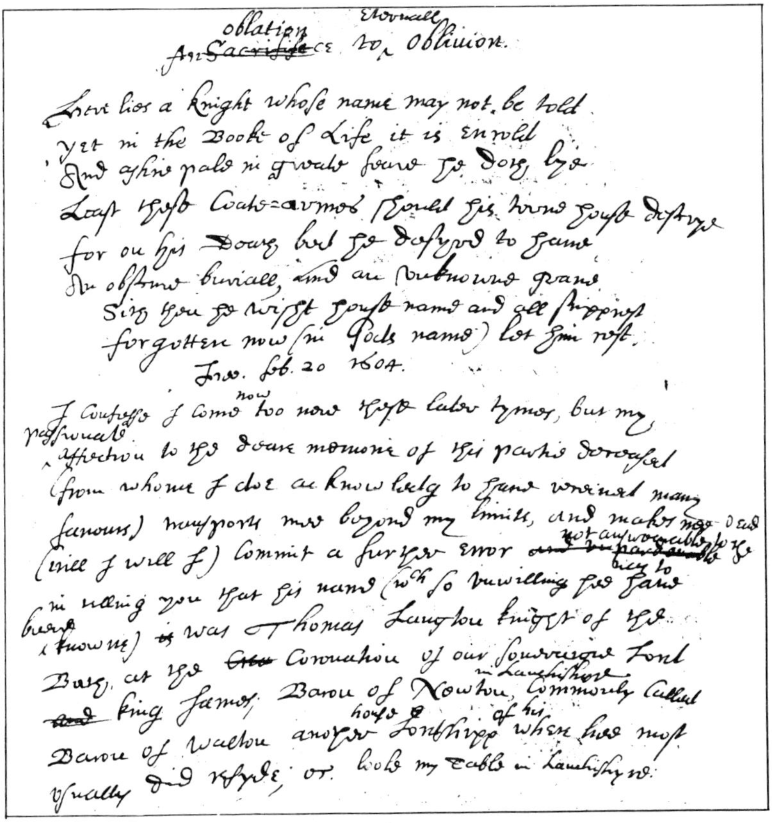

PLATE III   Weever's note on Sir Thomas Langton

VII

Ancient Funeral Monuments

❧∘☙

It will be as well to begin with the so-called 'original manuscript' (cf. p. 3). According to the Council Book of the Society of Antiquaries (14 February 1792), Weever's manuscripts were presented to the Council by William Southouse, who had been given them by a John Lane of Hillingdon, Middlesex, 'a relation of the family of the Weevers'. In 1792 Lane was dead, and Southouse knew no more. *A Catalogue of Manuscripts in the Library of the Society of Antiquaries of London* (1816) described the same manuscripts as follows:

> MS. 127. 'A Discourse of Funerall Monuments, of Burialls and kind of Buriall, of the Foundation and Fall of Religious Houses, of Religious Orders, and of other occurrences touched upon in the whole Passage of these intended Labours.' In folio. The original Manuscript of Weever's Funeral Monuments. Together with the rough draft for the Index to his printed Work. This Volume is marked A.—MS 128. A folio Book marked B. with the title on the Cover, 'The Rul'd Paper Booke.' Containing numerous Collections from Books and Manuscripts in the hand-writing of John Weever the Antiquary. At the beginning is an Index which does not appear to refer to this volume, but to Stow's Annals, &c.

MS. 127 consists of a rough draft for the index to *Funeral Monuments*, twenty-nine leaves, numbered (in modern pencil) to xxix; then 274 leaves, numbered 1–274 (in pencil), being notebooks and papers of various sizes, bound together. Most of the papers are $13\frac{1}{5} \times 8\frac{1}{2}''$.

MS. 128 consists of 424 leaves, numbered in pencil; notebooks and papers, various sizes, bound together.

Much of the material in these two volumes was printed in *Funeral Monuments*. Someone, probably in the eighteenth or nineteenth century, carefully collated the manuscripts and printed version, and inserted page references to the printed version in the manuscripts. This was not as simple as it sounds, as the printed text rarely follows the sequence of entries found in the manuscripts for many pages; the inscriptions, and Weever's comments on them, have been shuffled around, and much else has been added. Students of *Funeral Monuments* will find the anonymous collator's notes very helpful—not least because they also pinpoint most of the unpublished

sections in the manuscripts. Much of the unpublished material relates to
funeral inscriptions, etc., reserved by Weever for later volumes, but some
of it is personal, dealing with men Weever himself had known, as in the
case of two notes on Sir Thomas Langton (cf. p. 7). Here are two other
examples. First, Sir Thomas Gerard, the dedicatee of the fifth week of
Epigrammes:

> Under a sumptuous monument lies buried Sir Gilbert Gerard, Knight, some-
> times Attorney General to Queen Elizabeth and Master of the Rolls, who died
> the [blank]. And by him lies his son Sir Thomas Gerard sometimes Knight
> Marshal, and created by King James in the first of his reign Baron Gerard of
> Gerard's Bromley, the name of his magnificent house thereto adjoining and
> afterward made Lord President of Wales. He was a great warrior as having been
> with Henry the Fourth of France in all or most of his wars. He was at the
> expedition of Cadiz Colonel of a regiment of 750 men; he was in his young days
> an admirable tilter, in all points an absolute courtier, in all his days a bountiful
> housekeeper. He died the 7 of October 1617. Upon whom this epitaph was
> made—

As I suggest (p. 64), Weever's drafts of the epitaph indicate that he himself
wrote it. Second, a reference to the bishopric of London in 'this present
year of 1623 (in which that right reverend father in God and royal house-
keeper, George Mountain, Doctor of Divinity, doth right worthily rule
that sacred dignity'.[1] George Mountain, a Fellow of Weever's college, had
also been praised in *Epigrammes* (iv.19), but the later tribute was not
printed on page 356 of *Funeral Monuments*; just after being promoted to
the archbishopric of York, Mountain had died in 1628.

Two of these more personal and unpublished notes particularly interested me. The first concerns Sir Edward Stanley of Winwick (Lancashire)
and Tong (Shropshire), the dedicatee of *Faunus and Melliflora* ('To the
Right Valorous and excellent accomplished Gentleman, Master Edward
Stanley of Winwick, Esquire ... ': Stanley was knighted in 1603). It has long
been known that the funeral verses for Sir Edward and his father, Sir
Thomas Stanley, inscribed on their monument in Tong church were at-
tributed to 'William Shakespeare, the late famous tragedian', by Sir William Dugdale. E. K. Chambers and others have argued that they could not
be by Shakespeare, who died in 1616, whereas Sir Edward died in 1632. I
suggested recently that Sir Edward's tomb could have been erected before
he died, for, as Weever himself declared, it was not unusual in his day 'for
persons of especial rank and quality to make their own tombs and monuments in their life-time'.[2] Weever's unpublished note proves that Sir
Edward had done precisely this.

> [Tong here are many goodly monuments.] Sir Edward Stanley, Knight of the
> Bath, hath already made his own monument, whereon is the portraitures of
> himself, his wife, and his children, which were seven daughters and one son. She
> and her four daughters, Arbella, Mary, Alice and Priscilla, are interred under a

monument in the church of Walthamstow in Essex; Thomas his son died in his infancy, and is buried in the church of Winwick in 'Lanchishyre'; Petronella, Frances and Venetia are yet living.

> Ask who lies here, but do not weep:
> He is not dead, he doth but sleep.
> This stony register is for his bones,
> His fame is more perpetual than these stones.
> And his own goodness, with himself being gone,
> Shall live when earthly monument is none.
>
> Not monumental stone preserves our fame,
> Nor sky-aspiring pyramids our name.
> The memory of him for whom this stands
> Shall outlive marble and defacers' hands.
> When all to time's consumption shall be given
> Standley, for whom this stands, shall stand in heaven.[3]

The Stanley monument still remains in Tong church, though it has been moved from its original position. Weever did not know that its verses were associated with Shakespeare—presumably this attribution was not recorded in the church, and reached Dugdale from another source[4]—but Shakespeare's authorship becomes more plausible now that we are certain that the verses were written before Sir Edward Stanley's death in 1632.

The second unpublished note appears to be the first transcription of the verses on Shakespeare's tomb in Stratford upon Avon. Chambers said that 'the verses are transcribed in substantially, but not orthographically, their present form by Dugdale' in 1656.[5] Weever anticipated Dugdale by thirty years:

> #### Stratford upon Avon.
> Iudcio Pilum, Genio Socratem, Arte Maronem
>   Terra tegit, populus maeret, Olympus habet.
> Stay Passenger, why goest thou by so fast
> Read if thou canst whome envious death hath plac't
> Within this monument Shakespeare with whome
> Quick Nature dy'd whose name doth deck his Tombe
> far more then cost, sith all yt hee hath writt
> Leaves living Art but page to serve his witt.
>   ob An[n]o do[min]i 1616 AEtat. 53. 24 die April.
> Good frend for Iesus sake forbeare
> To digg the dust enclosed heare
> Blest bee ye man that spares these stones
> And curst bee hee that moves my bones.

In the margin, opposite 'Stratford upon Avon', someone—probably Weever—wrote 'Will[ia]m Shakespeare the famous poet', and, opposite the last two lines ('Blest ... bones'), 'vpo[n] the grave stone'. There are several minor discrepancies in this entry: 'Iudcio Pilum' for 'Ivdicio Pylivm' (in capitals), 'sith' for 'sieh' (where Weever corrected the stonecutter's error), and the date of Shakespeare's death (24 instead of 23

April). Shakespeare, of course, had been praised in Weever's *Epigrammes*. I have suggested that the two poets were acquainted, and that Weever probably saw Shakespeare's sonnets in or before 1599,[6] when they were passing round among his 'private friends'—so that it may at first seem surprising that Weever did not claim to have known Shakespeare when he copied his epitaphs. This has, however, no significance; he did not state that he had known Sir Thomas Gerard, Sir Edward Stanley or George Mountain—in his private notebooks, not intended for publication as they stood, such claims were unnecessary.

The 'original manuscript', then, comprises many different notebooks which were later bound together in two volumes; these were not really the original manuscript, but rather the collections upon which Weever drew when he prepared his lost 'fair copy' for the printer—though sometimes he copied whole paragraphs from the notebooks, still fidgeting with his text as he proceeded. The opening of Chapter I may serve as an example of his method (I omit some of his many deletions and insertions):

The first Chapter
Of Monuments in general.

A monument [general taken *interlined*] is a thing that is erected, made, or written, for a memorial to future ages, of some [memorable *deleted*] [remarkable *interlined*] and [laudable action *deleted*] fit to be transferred [for the worthiness thereof *deleted*] to future posterities: and thus generally taken [Books *deleted*] as well as Tombs or Sepulchres are called Monuments, according to this Ode of Horace ...

The printed version read as follows:

Chapter I.
Of Monuments in general

A Monument is a thing erected, made, or written, for a memorial of some remarkable action, fit to be transferred to future posterities. And thus generally taken, all religious Foundations, all sumptuous and magnificent Structures, Cities, Towns, Towers, Castles, Pillars, Pyramids, Crosses, Obelisks, Amphitheatres, Statues, and the like, as well as Tombs and Sepulchres, are called Monuments.

The first eighteen chapters (pp. 1–196) are a detachable part of the printed version, being an introduction to 'these intended labours'; Weever's methods changed, inevitably, when he reached the body of his book, but his textual fidgeting continued.

A remarkable feature of the whole book is its use of illustrative extracts from the poets. There are so many of them that the volume could be considered a poetical anthology, on the lines of *England's Parnassus*—continuing a tradition associated particularly with Weever's friends Robert Allott and Nicholas Ling. The poets include Homer, Pindar, Virgil, Ovid, Persius, Lucan, Statius, and also a surprising number

of medieval names. Chaucer and 'Piers Plowman' are two favourites, and
Harding's verse chronicle and Robert of Gloucester ('an old rhymer'
known to Weever from 'a manuscript in the Heralds' Office') come not far
behind, while Gower, Occleve and Lydgate also appear, not to mention
anonymous poems that Weever had found in the Cottonian Library and
elsewhere. Perhaps more surprisingly, in an antiquarian work, there are
many extracts from more recent poets—Skelton, Gavin Douglas, Churchyard, 'Martin Marprelate', Warner, Daniel, and, very often, Spenser
and Drayton. (The four last already received admiring tributes in the
Epigrammes.) But the greatest surprise is that really 'modern' poems and
translations are also included: Sir John Beaumont's *Bosworth-field* (1629;
S. R., 2 June), Thomas May's *Selected epigrams of Martial* (1629), and
May's *Continuation* of Lucan (1630; S. R., 3 March). May was a personal
friend ('thus exquisitely delivered in verse by my worthy friend the cont-
inuer of Lucan's historical poem', p. 24); Weever, however, though he
vigorously applauded his friends throughout his life, and did this frequently in *Funeral Monuments*, had another reason for larding his text with
poetical extracts. He wanted to remind the world that he was John Weever
the poet, a friend of poets; and that also explains why he took the unusual
step, for a living author, of placing verses below his engraved portrait.

  We are now ready to trace the writing of the final manuscript of *Funeral
Monuments*, which can be followed chronologically in Weever's text. To
assume that the printer's copy was ready when the book was entered in the
Stationers' Register (21 September 1630) would be folly; Weever's many
references to men 'now living' allow us to follow his progress and indicate
that the book was entered when the final copy was something like half
completed. We find 'Philip, Earl of Montgomery, now living, *Ann.* 1630'
(p. 284: Philip succeeded his brother William, the third Earl of Pembroke,
as fourth Earl of Pembroke on 10 April 1630); 'William Lord Cecil, Earl of
Salisbury ... now living, *Ann.* 1630' (p. 551); 'Robert Lord Rich ... now
living, *An.* 1631' (p. 627), and similar references to 1631 on pages 670, 674,
687, etc. The epistle 'To the Reader' (printed last, as was not unusual)
mentions that Sir Robert Cotton 'is now lately deceased', and dates his
death as 6 May 1631; the epistle itself is dated 28 May 1631. While the
printer may not have started on the book as early as September 1630, his
compositors clearly made faster progress than the author, who had to cut
himself short towards the end: 'much more might be said ... but I am called
for myself to the press' (p. 798); 'many more goodly tombs ... are in this
church ... the resemblances and figures whereof had been cut and de-
lineated, if the hastiness of the press would have permitted' (p. 853).

  If the surviving manuscripts may be taken as representative of 'penult-
imate copy', Weever's method in preparing his final fair copy seems to
have been as follows. He transcribed many short and some longer passages
direct from his own surviving manuscript notebooks, and at the same time

consulted other manuscripts—some of which have been identified—from which he again took whatever he found interesting. It seems to have been his intention at an early stage to quote liberally from English and other poets; I believe that he probably chose many of the scores of extracts from Chaucer, 'Piers Plowman', Spenser, Drayton, etc. when he wrote out his final fair copy, though earlier manuscripts contain some of these passages. He therefore had to keep his eye on many different manuscripts and printed books as he prepared the printer's copy.

More puzzling than Weever's mixing of funeral inscriptions and more general poetry, I think, is his method in moving from one place to another. One can understand his beginning with the diocese of Canterbury, and proceeding to Rochester, London, and Norwich; within each diocese, however, he zigzags unpredictably. Why, on page 266, go from Sibbertswood (6 miles north-west of Dover) to Ickham (5 miles east of Canterbury), to Chislehurst ('Here is the burial place of the Walsinghams': 45 miles west of Canterbury), to Monkton in the Isle of Thanet (7 miles north-east of Canterbury), to Wingham (2 miles from Ickham)? He was aware of the oddity:

> I may, perhaps, be found fault withal, because I do not chorographically and according as churches stand, near or further remote in one and the same lathe, hundred or wapentake, imprint and place the funeral monuments in this my book; but slip sometimes from one side of a county to another before I imprint an epitaph. ('To the Reader')

His explanation that he sometimes found nothing in adjacent churches (quoted p. 63, above), if that is what he meant, fails to account for the fact that he later retraced his steps and did make further discoveries. It is clear, as I have mentioned, that he could not have planned his journeys systematically; and, since the order of entries in the printed text often followed that of the notebooks, I conclude that in such cases it may reveal the true zigzag of his travels.

Was he equally unmethodical in his actual transcriptions? Weever's accuracy and reliability have been questioned by those who came after him. Henry Wharton set the tone in *Anglia Sacra* (2 vols., 1691): 'quod Weaverum attinet, is mortalium omnium infelicissimus cunctos fere numeros ex sepulchralibus titulis in farraginem suam descriptos vitiavit' (I, 668, ftn.; i.e. 'as far as Weever is concerned, he, the most unfortunate of all mortals, corrupted almost all the numbers copied from funeral inscriptions into his own nonsense'). Wharton (1664–95) was a young man of twenty-seven when he published this ungenerous verdict. As is usually agreed, some of Weever's numbers must be wrong; and it is possible that Wharton was able to check Weever's accuracy by comparing the printed text of 1631 with inscriptions still legible half a century later; yet Weever was, I believe, conscientious in his antiquarian transcriptions, and has been too harshly censured. Riding from church to church was time-consuming and expensive, and he had to rely, in part, on transcripts supplied by others. His book, moreover, created special problems for the printer, containing as it does so many quotations (sometimes with words missing, where the original could not be deciphered) in Anglo-Saxon, Middle English, Old French, Latin, etc. Weever drew attention to these difficulties in 'To the Reader': 'having had the helps and collections of many, my Reader may find errors in some, which hereafter I shall study to amend ... Many are the erratas, I am afraid, which will be found in the printing.'

Many of Weever's extracts, however, came not from tombs that have disappeared but from books that still survive, and so we can check his text against the original, with reassuring results. Apart from spelling and punctuation, which were often changed by printers at this time, Weever is usually so faithful to the author he transcribes that one can only wish that more of his contemporaries had been equally conscientious. Here are some random examples:—Weever, p. 1, 8 lines from Thomas May's *Selected Epigrams of Martial* (1629), 1 error ('nor' for 'no', l. 7); pp. 1–2, 5 lines from May's *Martial*, correct; p. 2, 8 lines from May's *Martial*, 2 errors ('AEgypt' for 'AEgypts', l. 2; 'said' for 'sad', l. 6); p. 3, 8 lines from May's translation of Lucan's *Pharsalia* (1627), 2 errors ('Thou' for 'That', l. 2; 'shalt' for 'shall', l. 6); p. 17, 6 lines from Holyday's *Persius* (1616, 1617), correct; p. 24, 8 lines from May's *Continuation* of Lucan (1630), correct; pp. 25–9, 172 lines from Sir John Beaumont's *Bosworth-field* (1629), 3 errors ('bodie' for 'bodies', l. 33; 'reuiues' for 'reuiewes', l. 38; 'thus' for 'this', l. 57).

When Weever copied from a good text, he seems to have done so with a high degree of accuracy. Some or all of the errors listed above will be misprints, of which he was aware. In the 'Epistle to the Reader' he says that 'the greatest I have met withal I have amended'—but at this time authors were rarely given the opportunity to proof-read every page. Now and then, however, his transcription appears to be faulty, as in the case of the epitaph for William Breke-spere:

> Here lieth *William Breke-spere* of London, sometime Merchant,
> Goldsmith and Alderman, the Common-wele attendant.
> Wyth *Margaryt* hys dawter, late wyff of *Suttoon*,
> And *Thomas* hur sonn yet liuyng vndyr Goddys tuitioon,
> The tenth of Iuyl he made hys transmigration.
> She disissyd in the yer of grase of Chrysts incarnatioon,
> A thowsand four hundryd threescor and oon.
> God assoyl her sowls whos bodys lye vndyr this stoon. (pp. 391–2)

It happens that the same epitaph was transcribed about fifteen years earlier by Nicholas Charles, Lancaster Herald, from the same tomb. 'In St Iohn Zacharies Church at the Lower end of Foster lane taken the 24. of July 1611 per me Nicholas Charles Lancaster ...'

Here lieth William Breakspere of
   London Marchant. Wth Margaret
   his daughter late wife of Iohn
Sutton Goldsmith and Alderman
The comonweale full well attendant
& Thomas her sonne yet liveing
   vnder Gods tuition
The 10: day of Iuyll she made
   her transmigration
God assoyle her soule whose bonys
   rest vnder this stone.
She deceased in the yeare of grace of christs
   Incarnation
A Thousand 4 Hundreth 3 score yeares & oone.[7]

As both versions of the epitaph derive from the same tomb, one has suffered badly in transmission. Nicholas Charles's manuscript is beautifully
meticulous, in text and illustrations, and therefore I suspect that his is the
more accurate version; an early draft of Weever's, however, proves that
the printer followed Weever's text exactly[8] (except for minor variations in
spelling and punctuation)—which suggests that in this instance Weever
was let down by someone else's faulty transcription. It would be quite
uncharacteristic of him to transpose words and lines, for, as my samples
have shown (they are representative of other passages I have checked)
almost the only errors in texts that we can compare with their immediate
sources are single-letter omissions or additions, the normal quota of misprints that we expect from seventeenth-century compositors. Weever, incidentally, had access to 'the collections of Nicholas Charles, Lancaster
Herald, deceased' (*Funeral Monuments*, p. 157).

Whether Weever himself should be held responsible for his errors, or the
manuscripts supplied by others, we cannot claim that his book is wholly
reliable. What, then, did he achieve? It is even more true than it was a
hundred years ago, when Sidney Lee made the point, that almost all of the
monuments described by Weever have since disappeared: here and there
we can compare the transcriptions preserved by other antiquaries, but
usually Weever's are all that has survived. We are indebted to him for
hundreds of epitaphs from the medieval and early modern period—not,
perhaps, 'absolute in their numbers', yet, on the other hand, not 'maimed
and deformed by the frauds and stealths of injurious impostors'. Given the
conditions in which he worked, we should be thankful that his texts are
reasonably sound.

The epitaph, admittedly, is not the highest form of literature. I would
not wish to make extravagant claims for *Funeral Monuments* because of
the number or quality of its epitaphs, even though the book undeniably
has its historical importance. I see it not as a haphazard collection of more

or less accurately transcribed funeral verses, but as one of a series of seventeenth-century books that includes Burton's *Anatomy of Melancholy*, Browne's *Religio Medici* and *Vulgar Errors*, as well as 'travel' books such as Coryate's *Crudities* (1611) and, a great favourite with Weever, George Sandys's *A relation of a journey begun anno Dom. 1610* (1615). In these books the author starts with a scientific or learned purpose, or, in the case of the travellers, a tale of strange adventures; their continuing appeal, however, depends not merely on the information they offer—it is the author's personality, his self-display, that also holds the reader. Compared with William Lambard (*A Perambulation of Kent*, 1576) or William Camden (*Britannia*, 1586 etc.), their seventeenth-century successors could be unashamedly self-indulgent—no one more so than John Weever.

To appreciate *Funeral Monuments*, therefore, we have to accept it as an intellectual ramble—a magnificently self-centred display of John Weever's passion for church history, poetry, pedigrees, and heraldry, 'intermixed and illustrated with variety of historical observations, annotations and brief notes' (title-page). The funeral monuments are his official subject, and he never loses sight of it: yet a reader who looks for an orderly discussion would quickly—to adapt Dr Johnson—hang himself. Not infrequently Weever wanders off in a digression, and cheerfully admits it: 'This chapter is grown much longer than I expected. Of which an end' (p. 176). It is an intensely personal book, verging at many points on the autobiographical.

I have already mentioned Weever's poetical extracts, and the fact that he claimed to know some of the poets concerned. His many acknowledgements to the heralds who had helped him are equally personal. There are also frequent references to his 'Lanchashire' background, in the verses beneath his engraved portrait and in many an irrepressible digression—for example, Kelley's conjuring at Walton le Dale (cf. p. 7), or the performance of plays 'in my country' (cf. p. 59). I have also mentioned that several of the friends and patrons addressed in the *Epigrammes* were to have figured in *Funeral Monuments*, and that some of these passages were scrapped, or held over for a later volume. Three of the seven dedicatees of *Epigrammes*, or their descendants, are named again in 1631: 'that honourable worthy gentleman, Sir Richard Molyneux of Sefton' (p. 234), 'Harrow on the Hill … now the habitation of a worthy Gentleman, Sir Gilbert Gerard' (p. 531), 'Sir Richard Hoghton of Hoghton Tower' (p. 760). An entry for a fourth, Sir Peter Legh, may have been intended on pp. 525–6; Sir Peter's wife, 'the virtuous Lady Margaret Legh', was buried in Fulham Church, and Weever had collected her epitaph but then excluded it⁹—probably because it was too modern. Unexpectedly, since Weever is supposed to be perambulating in the south-east of England, there are frequent references to Lancashire families, not least the Earls of Derby. 'The style, title and dignity of Lord Strange, James Stanley, eldest son and heir of William Earl of Derby (a gentleman of laudable endowments both of mind and body) now at this day happily enjoyeth'.[10]

Queens' College, Cambridge, must count as another personal, self-defining enthusiasm:

(1) Of this name and family is that orthodoxal sound divine, and worthy Master of Queens' College in Cambridge, John Mansell, Doctor of Divinity, and a general scholar in all good literature.

(2) Here lie interred the headless remains of John Fisher, Doctor of Divinity, sometime Bishop of Rochester, brought up a scholar in Cambridge; Master of our college (I mean Queens' College in Cambridge) and Chancellor of that University.

(3) The rector of this church at this time, as I am informed, is that reverend, learned divine and bountiful house-keeper, Robert Pearson, Doctor of Divinity, Archdeacon of Suffolk, sometime Fellow of Queens' College in Cambridge; to whom I am bound to acknowledge all thankfulness, he being in the same college my tutor.[11]

Such tributes—and perhaps most of the others—were no doubt intended to give pleasure to those concerned. Weever tried to make sure that they would, as far as his college was concerned, by sending it a presentation copy of the folio (inscribed 'To the learned and judicious view of the Master and Fellows of Queens' College in Cambridge John Weever presents these his imperfect labours.')

The folio, then, not only explores ancient funeral monuments but—typical of its age—it adds drama by adopting an emphatically personal point of view. The person (or persona?) defines himself through his relationships—with poets and poetry, heralds and antiquaries, Lancastrians, Cambridge men—and comes to life in his enthusiasms. He hears of wonders, and rushes off to see for himself. A man's body was found at Newport Pagnell in 1619 with 'the hollowness of every bone, as well ribs as other ... filled up with solid lead ... This I saw' (p. 30). He rummages in odd corners: 'And here let me tell you that amongst many letters of important affairs which I found in certain chandlers' shops of our parish, allotted to light tobacco pipes and wrap up pennyworths of their commodities ... I happened upon certain letters' (p. 80). He is warned off by churchwardens (cf. p. 64). We are invited to smile at the author's enthusiasm—and to bear with him when he becomes even more eccentric and glories in irrelevance:

Thus much have I spoken of a lawless court, for which I have neither law nor reason. For I am sure that this discourse is impertinent, and quite from the subject to which I have tied myself to treat of. Yet I hope these lines will not seem much unpleasing for my reader to peruse, when his mind is overcharged with dull, heavy and uncomfortable epitaphs. (pp. 605–6)

Whatever intrigues or amuses him finds a place, and reflects back on the omnipresent author. He is pleased with 'an old petition in rhyme ... upon which I lately happened in a very ancient manuscript in Sir Robert

Cotton's library ... The words are significant and modest, if you do not misinterpret.'

> *The petition of three poor nuns of Mergate.*
> We three poor nuns of Mergate
> Piteously complaineth to your good estate
> Of one Sir John of Whipsnade
> Who hath stopped our watergate
> With two stones and a stake.
> Help us, Lord, for Christ his sake! (pp. 585–6)

A petition is not a funeral monument, but no matter. Or could it be a hoax?

The author defines himself by what he chooses to include. His poetical extracts should be seen as conscious image-building, and also as another manifestation of Weever's long-established principle that it does no harm at all to praise one's friends. So many contemporary poets and other writers are applauded, often just in passing (e.g. 'the matchless and never enough admired pen of that famous, learned and eloquent knight, Sir Francis Bacon, not long since deceased', p. 476), that one wonders inevitably about two omissions. Neither Shakespeare nor Jonson is quoted—or mentioned. The explanation could be that modern dramatic poetry is excluded altogether, perhaps because it was considered too 'popular'. Yet Shakespeare and Jonson had both published non-dramatic verse; and, even if dialogue seemed inappropriate in an antiquarian work, it would have been possible to quote extracts from some of their longer speeches which would not have been self-evidently dramatic. The exclusion of two of the most celebrated poets of his age, both of whom Weever had admired, remains a puzzle. It is dangerous to draw inferences *a silentio*; I think, however, that Weever's silence must be meaningful, considering his friend-flattering propensities. Could it be that unforgivable things were said during the Poetomachia, in which all three poets had been involved?

Weever's folio, the repository of the research of two or three decades, must have been published in the summer of 1631. As far as he was concerned, it represented a major achievement. It was dedicated 'To the sacred and imperial majesty of our dread sovereign, the most magnificent, illustrious and puissant monarch, Charles' by 'his Highness' most lowly, and most loyal subject'—evidently a bid for recognition. Then, when the book was already on sale, someone had several afterthoughts. Why not a portrait of the author and an engraved title-page? A new sheet was added, with Weever's portrait (cf. Plate I) on the verso of the first leaf, and a more splendid title-page on the recto of the second, both engraved by Thomas Cecil. Why not a large paper edition? A few copies survive printed on larger, thicker paper—which made the book more expensive, and also more impressive. Would an index not be appropriate in a work of reference, and at the same time underline the author's extraordinary erudition? 'The Table' (or index) was printed, and is found in some of the

many recorded copies. The order in which these afterthoughts were im-
plemented is not certain, except that the engraved portrait and title-page
seem to have preceded the 'Table'. Weever's large paper presentation copy
inscribed to the Master and Fellows of Queens' College, Cambridge, included the engraved portrait and title-page, but not the 'Table': I assume
that the 'Table' had not yet been printed, for large paper copies with the
portrait, title-page and 'Table' are known.[12] It is not unreasonable to
ascribe these various attempts to give importance to the volume to its
humble author, conscious as he was that, amongst all the monuments and
memorials of mankind, 'books, or writings, have ever had the prehem-
inence' (p. 1). Did he suspect, even as he promised other volumes to follow,
that he had not long to live, that *Funeral Monuments* would have to be his
own monument? 'For I intend, God willing, hereafter to publish to the
view of the world as well the modern as the ancient memorials of the dead
throughout all his Majesty's foresaid dominions, if God spare me life; if
not, it is enough for me to have begun' ('To the Reader'). Within less than a
year the search for funeral monuments had ended: John Weever made his
will in February, and was dead by 29 March 1632.

VIII

Death and monument

When John Weever made his will on 16 February 1632, he claimed to be 'in sound mind and perfect health', a pleasing fiction that many a man still clings to on his death-bed. Probate was granted to his widow on 29 March 1632. The will is short, and may have been dictated by one who adopted the traditional preamble of wills for form's sake yet knew that he had not long to live:[1]

In Dei nomine Amen. I, John Weever of the parish of St James, Clerkenwell, in the county of Middlesex, gentleman, being in sound mind and perfect health of body, thanks be to almighty God, do make and ordain this my last will and testament in manner and form following. Imprimis, I commit my soul into the hands of the almighty, omnipotent and everliving God, in full assurance of everlasting salvation through the merits, death and passion of his only begotten Son, Jesus Christ, my alone saviour and redeemer. As for my body, I commit the same to Christian burial expecting a joyful resurrection. And for and concerning such worldly estate as God hath blessed me withal, I bequeath the same in manner and form following. Item, I give and bequeath unto my brother William Weever my black cloak with many laces. Item, I give to my sister Alice Cawthorne twenty shillings. Item, to my sister Anne Caton twenty shillings. Item, to my sister Isabel Holt twenty shillings. All which said several legacies to be given and paid to my brother and three sisters as aforesaid, my will is shall be given and paid by Anne my dearly beloved wife within one year next after my decease. And I do make and ordain my said wife Anne Weever the sole executrix of this my last will and testament. And I do make and appoint my nephew William Cawthorne overseer of this my will, to whom I give twenty shillings to buy him a ring. Item, I give and bequeath my lease of my house in Gray's Inn Lane, now in the tenure of George Dawson, and the lease of my house in Clerkenwell wherein I now dwell, together with all goods, chattels, moneys, plate, household stuff and all the rest of my personal estate whatsoever, not before bequeathed, to my said executrix Anne Weever, my beloved wife. And lastly I hereby revoke and make void all former wills and testaments by me made. In witness whereof I have hereunto set my hand and seal the sixteenth day of February in the seventh year of the reign of our sovereign lord Charles, by the grace of God King of England, Scotland, France and Ireland, defender of the faith &c Annoque domini 1631 [i.e. 1632, new style]. John Weever. Sealed and signed in the presence of John Witt and [   ] Gardner.

Endorsed: 29 Martij 1632 Iurata executrix.

Probatum apud London ... xxix Martij A° domini 1632 ...
Anne Weaver.

As already explained (p. 58), the Anne Weaver of St James, Clerkenwell, who made her will in 1647 was almost certainly John's widow and executrix.

In the name of God Amen. I, Anne Weaver, of the Parish of St James, Clerkenwell, in the county of Middlesex, widow, being aged and weak in body but of good and perfect mind and memory, thanks be therefore given to almighty God; and having had long experience of the certainty of death of all creatures living, and the uncertainty of the time thereof, do therefore this fifth day of May in the year of our Lord God one thousand six hundred forty and seven—make my last will and testament in manner and form following. That is to say, first and principally I do willingly and with a free heart render and give again into the hands of my Lord God and Creator my spirit, which he of his fatherly goodness gave unto me when he first fashioned me in my mother's womb, making me a living and reasonable creature. Nothing doubting but that for his infinite mercy's sake, abundantly set forth in the precious blood of his dearly beloved son, Jesus Christ our Lord and only Saviour and Redeemer, he will when this life is ended receive my soul into his glory, and place it in the company of heavenly angels and blessed saints to all eternity. And as concerning my body, even with a good will and free heart I give it over, commending it to the earth whereof it came, to be decently interred according to the discretion of my executor hereinafter named, verily believing according to that article of my faith, at the great day of the general resurrection when we shall appear before the judgement seat of Christ, I shall receive the same again by the mighty power of God wherewith he is able to subdue all things to himself, not a corruptible, mortal, weak and vile body as it is now, but an uncorruptible, immortal, strong and perfect body, in all points like unto the glorified body of my Lord and Saviour Jesus Christ. And now as touching the disposition of that small estate which God hath lent and left me in this life, I dispose thereof as followeth, videlicet, imprimis, I give and bequeath unto my brother Paul Onion [Vnnyon] the sum of five pounds of lawful money of England, to be paid unto him by ten shillings every quarter of a year, from and after the time of my decease, until it be satisfied according to my true intent and meaning. Item, I also give and bequeath unto my said brother the bedstead and featherbed whereon I usually lie, together with two feather bolsters, two pillows, two blankets, one green rug, and the curtain's valance and mat thereunto belonging, and likewise four pair of sheets, four tablecloths, one dozen of napkins, one drawing table standing in the hall, one green darnex [cf. OED, dornick] carpet, and two joint-stools, hoping that as this is the last gift which he is to expect from me, so he will make much of it, for my sake and his own. Item, I give and bequeath unto my loving friend and ancient neighbour, Mr Thomas Baker, apothecary, the sum of twenty shillings to bestow on what he thinketh good, to keep in remembrance of me. All the rest of my goods and chattels whatsoever, whereof I shall die possessed (my debts, funeral expenses and legacies being paid and discharged) I fully and freely give and bequeath unto my kind friend Thomas Palmer of Clerkenwell aforesaid, bricklayer, in acknowledgement of the love and care which he hath shown to me and had of me. And I make the said Thomas Palmer

sole executor of this my last will, and the before named Thomas Baker overseer
hereof. In witness whereof I the said Anne Weaver have to this my testament,
containing with this sheet four sheets of paper, set my hand and seal the day and
year before written.

Signed sealed and published   the mark of the said
... in the presence of   Anne Weaver
us, Edward Gregory, Scr[ivener]
John Bayly

It is strange that Anne left no bequests to anyone named in John's
will—though perhaps not quite so strange if one recalls that they appear to
have been a childless couple. In such circumstances a widow may drift
away from her former husband's family. It is just possible, of course, that
more then one John and Anne Weever lived in St James, Clerkenwell, at
the same time, but it seems unlikely if we narrow the odds by stipulating
that then both childless couples, with the same Christian names, lived in
the same parish at the same time and belonged to the same social class.[2]
Anne Weever had her own seal, which survives intact on her will; unfortunately, John Weever's seal has crumbled on the original of his will—had
it not done so it might have clinched the case that Anne was John's widow.
As she made her mark instead of signing her name, the fact that the scriven-
er spelt her name 'Weaver', not Weever, can have no significance.

Shortly after John Weever's death a 'monument' was erected for him in
his parish church with verses in his honour. The monument has disappeared, but the verses survive. Different accounts of the monument were
printed at various times, with additional information about Weever that
may or may not be correct. The author who grieved that so many monuments have been 'torn away and pilfered, by which inhuman, deformid-
able act the honourable memory of many virtuous and noble persons
deceased, is extinguished', would certainly expect us to search for his
'memorials' and to restore them to the world.

Within a year or so of Weever's death, the verses on his monument were
printed in Anthony Munday's edition of Stow's *Survey of London* (1633),
in a section dealing with St James, Clerkenwell (p. 900):

> *Upon my very worthy friend, Master*
> *John Weaver, a learned antiquary.*
> Weaver, who laboured in a learned strain
> To make men, long since dead, to live again,
> And with expense of oil and ink did watch
> From the worm's mouth the sleeping corse to snatch,
> Hath by his industry begot a way
> Death (who insidiates all things) to betray;
> Redeeming freely, by his care and cost,
> Many a sad hearse which time long since gave lost,
> And to forgotten dust such spirit did give
> To make it in our memories to live.

Where Death destroyed when he had power to save
In that he did not seek to rob the grave,
For wheresoe'er a ruined tomb he found
His pen hath built it new out of the ground.
'Twixt earth and him this interchange we find,
She hath to him, he been to her like kind.
She was his mother, he, a grateful child,
Made her his theme in a large work compiled,
Of funeral reliques, and brave structures reared
On such as seemed unto her most endeared.
Alternately a grave to him she lent,
O'er which his book remains a monument.
Master Weaver upon himself.
Lancashire gave me breath.
   And Cambridge education,
Middlesex gave me death,
   And this church my humation,
And Christ to me hath given
A place with him in heaven.
Obiit Anno AEtat. suae 56.

As already stated, Whittle claimed in 1837 that 'a monument was erected at the cost of John Skillicorne, armiger of Preston, being his executor ... '.[3] Weever, however, appointed his wife Ann Weever his executrix, 'cui commissa fuit administratio omnium et singulorum bonorum' (29 March 1632); and, as we now know that Anne Weever lived for many more years, it is unlikely that John Skillicorne was ever her husband's executor. Could he, then, have written the verses 'Upon my very worthy friend, Master John Weaver'? The Skillicornes, according to Edward Baines, the great Lancashire antiquary, 'held the manor of Preese, in the reign of Henry VIII; and William Skillicorne was living here in 43 Elizabeth ... [From Flower's *Visitation*, 1567] it appears that ... William himself, who had a brother John, married Jane, daughter of Sir Thomas Houghton, of Houghton'.[4] Preese or Preesall is close to Stalmine, where Weever's uncle, Henry Butler, owned property—so Whittle's story, linking Weever and John Skillicorne, might have some truth in it. It is therefore disappointing to have to report that in a different section of Stow's *Survey* of 1633, one also concerned with St James, Clerkenwell, there is an account of the monument of Thomas Bedingfield, Esq., who died on 11 August 1613, and that it ends—'This Monument was made and placed here, at the cost and charges of John Skillicorne, Esquire, being his Executor' (p. 486). I suspect that Whittle's papers were not as tidy as they should have been, and that this note on Bedingfield's monument was wrongly attached to the notes on Weever's.

Whittle's text of the verses on Weever omitted two lines, 'Where Death destroyed ... rob the grave', and the same two lines are missing from Edward Hatton's text printed in *A New View of London* (1708). Perhaps

Whittle consulted Hatton, or some other authority apart from Stow. Whittle also differed from Stow in a number of minor variants: 'his' for 'this' (l. 5), 'costs' for 'cost' (l. 7), 'has' for 'hath' (l. 14), etc. When one compares Whittle's extract from Weever's epistle 'To the Reader' with the original it is again disappointing that what purports to be Weever's text turns out to be a loose paraphrase:

> He says 'that he had been taken up in divers churches, by the churchwardens of the parish, and not suffered to write the epitaphs, or take views of the monuments, as I much desired—for that I wanted a commission, which would have greatly encouraged me, for Henry 8th, did grant license to John Leyland, in order that he might effectually prosecute his antiquarian researches.'

It follows, I think, that all of Whittle's observations must be treated with caution.

Whether the shorter epitaph, 'Master Weaver upon himself', was inscribed on the monument or found elsewhere is not clear. We may assume that Anthony Munday, who added recent epitaphs and other material to the second and third editions of the *Survey of London* (John Stow, the author, having died in 1605), must have known Weever, since he shared the same enthusiasms and transcribed verses from the same London churches. Munday died on 10 August 1633, aged eighty, and his own epitaph was printed in the 1633 edition of the *Survey of London* (p. 869), a work 'enlarged by the care and diligence of A. M.[unday] in the year 1618' and 'completely finished by the study and labour of A. M. H. D. and others' in 1633: Munday's study and labour overlapped with Weever's own, and Munday could have been given Weever's last poem, the epitaph 'upon himself', by the author or his widow. Weever, it will be noted, simply adapted the verses already printed in *Funeral Monuments* (cf. p. 4). The final version must have been composed as he lay on his death-bed, and the confidence of the last two lines ('And Christ to me hath given / A place with him in heaven') is therefore all the more remarkable.

What happened to Weever's monument? In *A History of the Society of Antiquaries* (Oxford, 1956) Joan Evans wrote that in the 1780s the Society's 'only activity in preservation was for Weever's monument in the church of St James, Clerkenwell, which was kept when the church was pulled down and replaced in the new church. Council, 21 Apr. 1787'.[5] The vicar of St James (the Revd J. Roberts) tells me, however, that Weever's monument, 'does not appear anywhere in the present building', and cites the following passage from W. J. Pinks, *The History of Clerkenwell* (1865), concerning Weever's 'monument', which seems to have been a mere tablet:

> When the church was taken down, the Society of Antiquaries, with a very proper zeal for the preservation of this tablet, ordered a diligent search to be made for it, but without success, as it had been taken from the church a few years previously by some person or persons unknown. (p. 42)

How can we square this with what is said by Joan Evans? Referring to the
Council Book of the Society of Antiquaries, I think that she perhaps mis-
read a good intention as a good deed. The Minutes record that E. Baker
wrote to the Society, stating that 'an advertisement in the public papers'
asked those interested 'to remove any monuments belonging to them'
before St James is pulled down; Mr Baker observed 'that there is in that
church a small monument to the memory of that great and learned antiquarian, Weever'; 'as it is most probable, none of his family is now exist-
ing', the Society is urged to preserve the monument. The Council recommended the task to 'Mr. Gough', who 'kindly undertook to execute the
same'. Either the tablet had been removed 'a few years previously', as
Pinks asserted, or Mr Gough did as he was asked without, however, re-
placing the tablet in the new church (which, strictly speaking, was not
what he agreed to do. He may have preserved it elsewhere).

Pinks's *History of Clerkenwell* was able to give detailed information
about Weever's monument, which supplements Whittle's account:

> In the old church was a marble tablet, surrounded by a black border, affixed to
> the first pillar on the right, entering the chancel, on which was inscribed the
> following encomiastic lines in praise of an old antiquary, John Weever, the
> well-known author of a book on 'Funeral Monuments', who died in the reign of
> Charles I, and was buried under a pew near the pillar against which this mem-
> orial of him was placed:—
> 'UPON A VERY WORTHY FRIEND, MR. JOHN WEEVER, A
> LEARNED ANTIQUARY'.

(Pinks then printed the lines, 'Weever, who laboured in a learned strain',
already quoted.)[6] Pinks's account of the monument tallies closely with that
given by Edward Hatton in *A New View of London* (2 vols., 1708), though
Pinks had additional information:

> On a Pillar, at the W. end of the Church, are these Lines on a Table, with a black
> Frame fronting Nd, in Memory of the learned Antiquary *Mr. John Weever*,
> here buried.
> Weever *who labour'd in a learned Strain* ...

Weever's statement, that books and writings 'have ever had the prehem-
inence' above tombs, structures and other 'remembrances',[7] certainly
proves to be correct where he himself was concerned.

A photographic reproduction of Weever's *Epigrammes* (1599), together with an introduction and commentary

INTRODUCTION

In this introduction to the *Epigrammes*, and in the notes that follow, my concern is historical, rather than literary or critical: that is, I discuss the printing and proof-reading of the poems, their dates and arrangement in seven 'weeks', and in the notes I try to identify the persons and events alluded to, with only occasional comments on other obscurities. The reader will be disappointed if he looks for an historical account of satire and epigram, or for an appreciation of Weever's excellence in this genre. I hope that I have already shown that I do not overrate Weever as a poet, but consider him important for other reasons.

Much of the essential historical information needed by readers of the *Epigrammes* will be found in the preceding chapters. These dealt with Weever's friends in Lancashire, Cambridge and London, with the significance of the Privy Council decree of 1 June 1599, banning satires and epigrams, and with the career of Valentine Simmes, Weever's printer. So I begin with a description of the two surviving copies of the *Epigrammes*, and of the evidence of press-correction.

Neither of the two known copies is perfect. The more complete of the two, in the Bodleian Library, Oxford (Malone 904), is a small octavo, collating A-G^8, and lacks leaf A8. The other, in the Harvard University Library, lacks leaves A1, A2, A8 and G8. First and last leaves often come away from older books; it seems, however, that leaf A8 was removed deliberately (and leaf A7 may have been tipped in in one or both copies).[1] Why? Since every 'week' except the first is preceded by a dedication or epistle, we may assume that both copies—hereafter O and H—at one stage contained, on leaf A8, a dedication for week i. I suspect that this dedication was addressed to Sir Richard Hoghton, and that Weever later decided to dedicate the whole book, not just week i, to Hoghton; if so, the printer misunderstood his instructions. All the other dedications, it will be observed, occupy a single page, and are of approximately the same length;

the Hoghton dedication is longer and spreads across two pages. My guess is that when Weever finally prepared his manuscript for the printer, he had the bright idea that he might please seven patrons, and prefixed a 'dedication' to each of the seven weeks; then, as an afterthought, he decided to dedicate the whole volume to Hoghton, composed a more weighty dedication, and possibly a new one addressed to someone else which was to go with week i. The printer, however, mindlessly set up the cancelled dedication to Hoghton on leaf A8—hence the need to remove this leaf. It is only a guess: but there are other signs (cf. p. 88) that the printer misunderstood Weever's last-minute instructions.

The variants in Simmes's octavo are few and mostly trivial. (1) C5a '*In obitum sepulcrum Gullionis.*' (O), '*In obitum Gullionis.*' (H); (2) C5b(Epig. 23, line 6). 'mã' (O), 'man' (H); (3) E7a 'sir Thomas Gerrard knight, Marshall' (O), 'sir Thomas Gerard knight, Marshiall' (H); (4) E8b '*Epig. 5*', '*Epig. 6*' (O), '*Epig. 7*', '*Epig. 8*' (H). Some turned letters are also corrected (E2b, '*Sterou*' (H); G1b, line 2, 'paiue' (H)). The printer rather than the author must be responsible for these press-corrections, for Weever would have removed the intrusive comma in (3): Sir Thomas Gerard was a 'Knight Marshal'. And Weever would surely have noticed other, more serious errors.

On the date of composition of the *Epigrammes*, McKerrow gives us a good start:

[Weever] must have been born in 1575 or 1576, and as in the verses to the readers prefixed to the present work, he claims that his 'tender-blushing youth' has not yet known 'twenty twelve months', it has been customary to regard the epigrams as having been written in 1595 ... Examination shows, however, that this is certainly not the date of the work as a whole, and probably only a small part of it was written so early. Even this epistle to the reader cannot, at least in its present form, be dated earlier than 1598, for it contains an undoubted allusion to Marston's *Scourge of Villany*, first published in that year ... Further, when we turn to the Epigrams themselves we find one [ii.21] containing the date 1598, and another [vi.23] referring to the death of Spenser, which took place in January, 1598/9 ... If the Thomas Egerton on whose death there is an epigram [vii.11] was the son of Sir T. Egerton, Baron Ellesmere, that epigram at least must have been written later than August, 1599, when he was killed in Ireland.[2]

McKerrow concluded that the epigrams were 'written at various times during four or five years, the majority dating probably from 1597–8'.

Several other points must now be mentioned. (1) In his verses 'to the readers' Weever not only claims that he has not known 'twenty twelve months' but describes himself as a Cambridge man, one who has not plashed in the Isis:

Nor have I spent in Troynovant my days
Where all good wits, some say, are crowned with bays.

This can only mean, I think that Weever wrote the poem 'to the readers' some years before his arrival in London in 1598 (cf. p. 21), but added the last verses, referring to Marston, in 1598 or 1599. (2) In a prose epistle to the readers Weever apologised for the belated appearance of the epigrams, 'being for one year penned, and in another printed'. This agrees with '159 and 8' in ii.21, and with the rueful acknowledgement in i.7 that there had been delays and disappointments before Weever's first book finally appeared. Most of the epigrams must have been written by 1598. (3) The apology to 'the generous readers', probably Weever's final addition to his book, must have been written near the end of 1599 (see notes on A7a, 'this year of jubilee', and on A2, dedication). (4) And, as McKerrow said, some epigrams must be assigned to 1599—the question is, how many?

I thought that I had answered this last question when I noticed that the *Epigrammes* divide into seven 'weeks' that consist of twenty-three poems each. That, at any rate, appears to have been Weever's final intention, even though the number of epigrams in each week, in the book as printed, is i, 23; ii, 25; iii, 23; iv, 23; v, 24; vi, 25; vii, 17.

> Taking into account that two epigrams in week ii are blanks [numbers 3 and 10] ... we find the totals to be 23, 23, 23, 23, 24, 25, 17. (The fourth week in fact includes an unnumbered epigram, after iv.3 ...). If we now add to week vii the two deleted epigrams from week ii, the unnumbered one from week iv, and the three from weeks v and vi in excess of twenty-three, we discover that the result is seven weeks each containing exactly twenty-three poems—and this, I take it, was Weever's final intention.[3]

Since Weever himself explained that his book was intended for 1598 and was 'ready made' more than once, it seemed that some verses written after 1598 (viz. vi.23, vii.11) were included in weeks v–vii, and that weeks i–iv were completed by 1598: but, as we shall see, new facts have come to light and so neat a chronology is no longer acceptable.

Before I return to chronology, let us look more closely at the symmetry of the seven 'weeks' and at the volume's printing history. Two books published in 1598 probably inspired Weever to arrange his epigrams as he did: Thomas Bastard's *Chrestoleros* or 'seven books of epigrams' (S. R., 3 April 1598), and William Rankins's *Seven Satires* 'applied to the week' (S. R., 3 May 1598)—both no doubt influenced by Du Bartas. The decision to assign exactly twenty-three epigrams to each of the seven weeks may only have been taken at the very last moment, however, in 1599: without the poems on the deaths of Upcher, Spenser and Egerton (iv.3; vi.23; vii.11) the numbers would not have been right. I suspect that when Simmes, the printer, at last found time for the book, Weever hurriedly wrote out the dedications (those for Hoghton, Warren and Halsall cannot be earlier than June and July 1599, when the three were knighted), and at the same time gave Simmes instructions for rearranging the poems in seven weeks, each consisting of twenty-three epigrams; Simmes, being less interested in symmetry than in finishing quickly, failed to carry out all of the author's wishes but left enough clues to allow us to guess what they were.

Quite apart from the profusion of obvious misprints, the *Epigrammes* suffered from the printer's quite exceptional carelessness. The dedications have been mentioned already. It is also probable that when a week's first epigram addresses one of the seven dedicatees, the epigram and dedication should have been printed together, as in week ii (dedication and ii.1 addressed to Robert Dalton, Esq.). In weeks v–vii the arrangement is as follows: v, dedication, Sir Thomas Gerard; v.1, Sir Peter Leigh; vi, dedication, Sir Cuthbert Halsey; vi.1, 'Ad Richard Houghton Militem'; vii, dedication, Sir Peter Leigh; vii.1, Sir Thomas Gerard. The dedications to Gerard and Leigh should surely be switched around, and perhaps the Hoghton epigrams (vi. 1, 3, 4) were at one stage meant to begin the volume, just as a fourth Hoghton epigram helps to close it (vii.16. Note that this poem reverts to vi.1: 'my pen' and 'thy gold-gilded tower' are picked up again in the poet's 'golden pen').

No doubt Weever himself was partly to blame. And he too must be held responsible for the use of outdated titles ('Ad Richardum Houghton Militem', vi.1, vii.16: compare Peter Leigh and Thomas Gerard, v.1, vii.1) which do not tally with the dedications, where these newly created knights were addressed correctly. The printer, however, made little or no attempt to tidy his text, and introduced many more inconsistencies. (a) Weeks i–iv print the first epigram of each week on the recto of the leaf, and in i–iii the preceding verso is blank; weeks v and vii print the first epigram on a verso. (b) Weeks i–iv all end with the word '*Finis*', whereas v and vi omit it (it reappears in vii because this is the end of the volume). (c) The 'E' in 'Epigram' is always an italic or swash capital in i–iv; in v–vii a roman capital frequently occurs as well. Many other little irregularities (e.g. in the catch-words, and in the use of stops in the epigram headings) prove, at the very least, the printer's indifference to the book's appearance, and perhaps that the compositors changed or the printing was interrupted. My photographic reproduction of *Epigrammes* will help readers to check the book's printing history for themselves; those who do so will agree that we cannot claim for it the 'careful workmanship' that Ferguson thought, in general, characteristic of a Simmes publication.[4]

I argued in *Shakespeare: the 'lost years'* that the irregularities in the *Epigrammes* indicate 'different textual origins' for weeks i–iv and v–vii. Though no longer convinced of this, I think it intriguing that a special ornament was placed at the end of week iv; taken together with (b) above, it suggests that the compositor regarded weeks i–iv as a unit, and Weever's text or texts could have given him this idea. Yet while the printer's copy was no doubt messy and imperfectly finalised, the more closely we examine the book's 'irregularities' the more likely it seems that most of them resulted from haste and carelessness in the printing-house. That means that we have to abandon the hypothesis (cf. p. 88) that the epi-

grams in weeks i-iv were written by 1598, and that the few additional
epigrams composed in 1599 were inserted in weeks v, vi or vii—a hypothesis that has lapsed in any case with the discovery that Captain John
Upcher, whose decease is lamented in iv.3, died between March and
August 1599.[5]

Nevertheless, even if we now know that Weever commemorated three
deaths that occurred in 1599, almost all the other datable epigrams belong
to earlier years, and we may reasonably conclude that they were 'ready
made' in 1598. The new evidence about Weever's Cambridge circle (Chapter III, above) confirms McKerrow's opinion that the epigrams were 'written at various times during four or five years', though more of them probably antedated 1598 than he believed. Does that help at all in the dating of
iv.22, the epigram to Shakespeare? This is important as the first extant
poem addressed to the dramatist, but would be even more important if it
was written before Francis Meres praised Shakespeare so enthusiastically
in *Palladis Tamia* late in 1598. (Meres dated his dedication 19 October
1598.) For, while Meres mentioned Shakespeare's 'sugared sonnets among
his private friends', without giving any more detail, Weever made iv.22 a
'Shakespearian' sonnet; of around 160 epigrams in his collection, most of
them between four and twenty lines in length, one, and only one, is fourteen lines long and rhymes abab, cdcd, efef, gg. This can only mean one
thing—that Weever had seen some of Shakespeare's sonnets, and wished
to signal to others in the know that he had enjoyed this privilege.

Weever's sonnet, I think, makes a claim of some sort. Could it be that he
was one of the 'private friends'? Or had he read *The Passionate Pilgrim*
('By W. Shakespeare') which also came out in 1599 and perhaps preceded
the *Epigrammes*? (The exact dates of publication of the two books are
unknown.) As I have explained elsewhere,[6] only eight of the twenty poems
in *The Passionate Pilgrim* were fourteen-line sonnets, and only four of the
eight were by Shakespeare: anyone as familiar with the London literary
scene as Weever appears to have been would soon hear that some of the
poems in *The Passionate Pilgrim* were reprinted from Barnfield, Weelkes,
Griffin and Marlowe, and would be suspicious about the attribution of the
volume as a whole. Shakespeare was 'much offended' with the publisher
who 'presumed to make so bold with his name' when *The Passionate
Pilgrim* was later reissued,[7] so we may assume that he also repudiated the
book as soon as he heard of it in 1599. In 1599, before the sonnets as a
whole had been published, there was no good reason to consider the 'Shakespearian' sonnet Shakespeare's characteristic form, and Weever's choice
of this particular form, for just one epigram out of around 160, may indeed
imply that he had seen a manuscript of the 'sugared sonnets among his
private friends'.

On the other hand, I have argued (p. 27) that Weever and Meres belonged to the same literary circle in London. It remains to add that *Palladis*

Tamia and the *Epigrammes* appear to echo one another in at least two places: each echo consists of just a single word, but one sufficiently unusual to give us pause. Meres praised 'mellifluous & honey-tongued Shakespeare' (p. 281 b), and Weever addressed 'Honey-tongued Shakespeare' (iv.22); the word was not new—see 'honey-tongued Boyet' in *Love's Labour's Lost* (V.2.334)—and, on its own, might be dismissed as a coincidence. Meres, however, also said that 'Warner in his absolute *Albion's England* hath most admirably penned the history of his own country' (p. 281 b), and Weever promised Warner 'This be thy praise: thy *Albion's* absolute' (vi.13).[8] Now some or all of the epigrams addressed by Weever to London's literary stars could have been added to his collection after he arrived in London, including the one on Shakespeare. (The epigram on Marston and Jonson, vi.11, probably dates from late 1598 or 1599; in *Palladis Tamia* Meres could not name 'the author of *Pygmalion's Image* and *Certain Satires*' (p. 277 b), but Weever, it seems, knew of Marston's authorship and therefore praised him as another Horace.) If, however, Weever's epigram on Shakespeare was composed after the publication of *Palladis Tamia*, it is strange that he wrote '*Romea Richard*; more whose names I know not', when Meres had actually named twelve plays. The two poems and two plays named by Weever were all published in or before 1597; it remains possible that Weever wrote about Shakespeare at Cambridge, having read some of the plays but not seen them performed in London—and that Meres echoed Weever, who clearly tried very hard to make himself and his poems known in 1598–9. The literary circle to which Weever attached himself in London was no doubt asked to read his poems and help to get them published; Meres, as we have seen, was aware of unpublished poetry; *Palladis Tamia* appeared after 19 October 1598, and Weever claimed that the *Epigrammes* (1599) were 'for one year penned, and in another printed'. Here we should recall Weever's assertion that he wrote the 'first true *Oldcastle*', one that had to wait for two years before it was printed (cf. above, p. 31), i.e. one that preceded the first defence of Oldcastle to win public recognition; and that the play that preceded Weever's 'first true *Oldcastle*' was partly written by Michael Drayton, who could have borrowed the idea from his friend's unpublished poem. It by no means follows that what was written first was also printed first: an unsatisfactory conclusion for those who wish to know whether Meres or Weever praised Shakespeare first, but at least it acknowledges that there is a problem. We simply do not know when Weever wrote the sonnet-epigram on Shakespeare.

Nevertheless, since Alexander Hoghton, Esq. (a previous owner of Hoghton Tower, and the uncle of Sir Richard Hoghton) named 'William Shakeshafte' as one of his servants in 1581, and recommended Shakeshafte to Sir Thomas Hesketh together with his play-clothes and musical instruments, the inclusion of Weever's sonnet to Shakespeare in a volume that,

we now see, also manages to celebrate so many other members of the
Hoghton family and its connections, need not be a mere coincidence. If
Shakeshafte was Shakespeare, and served Alexander Hoghton as an assist-
ant schoolmaster and player, as I have suggested, Sir Richard may well
have been one of Shakespeare's pupils, at the age of ten or so, in 1580–81.
The tradition that Shakespeare served the Hoghtons in his youth, handed
down within the family from father to son, must have originated with Sir
Richard; unless we dismiss it as fabricated—which seems unreasonable, in
so far as the tradition antedates the theory that Shakeshafte was
Shakespeare—Sir Richard Hoghton is not only interesting in himself but
also important for students of Shakespeare. The 'sonnet' on Shakespeare
may well have been written, among other things, to please Sir Richard, the
principal dedicatee of the *Epigrammes*.[9]

THE EPIGRAMMES

The following reproduction of the Bodleian Library copy, by kind permission, from a microfilm supplied by the Library, is approximately two-
thirds of the original size. The rectangular outlines indicate the area of the
openings; that is, from page 93 I reproduce four pages on every page.
Signatures have been added in the bottom left-hand corner of each
opening.

EPIGRAMMES
in the oldeſt cut, and
neweſt faſhion.

A

*twiſe ſeuen houres (in ſo many
weekes) ſtudie*

No longer (like the faſhion) not vn-
like to continue.

The firſt ſeuen.

Iohn Weeuer.

Sit voluiſſe, Sat valuiſſe.

At London
Printed by *V.S.* for *Thomas Buſhell*, and are to be
ſold at his ſhop at the great north doore
of *Paules* 1599

A1a

To the Right Worſhipfull and
worthie honoured Gentleman ſir Richard Houghton of Houghton Tower,
Knight : Iuſtice of Peace, and Quorum : High
*Sheriffe of Lanchſhire,&c. Adorned with all
giftes, that valour may giue, or
vertue gaine.*

Nowing, and admiring (Right Wor.)
the generall applauſe, and loue which
you haue of your cuntrie, wonne (no
doubt) by your vertues,ſeated in a hart
of curteſie: And the experience which
many ſchollers haue had of your kindneſſe,neuer to be
forgotten, but with vngratefulneſſe: perſwade me you
wil animate my yong Muſe, and vouchſafe to per-
uſe the fruites, of my not curious nor careleſſe ſtudies: albeit I muſt confeſſe farre vnworthie your Wor:
view; Vnleſſe,(like the wiſeſt ſenator)you would haue

A 2   your

A1b, A2a

The Epiſtle Dedicatorie.

your ſerious affaires intermedled with diuers delights,
to driue away the tedsouſneſſe of time. Then(moſt
bountifull Mecœnas)if you fauour the effeEt of my labour,jt will ſerue you for a ieaſt, to refreſh your wea-
ried mind,continually exrciſed in matters concerning
the common wealth. And thus I commend my
Booke to your mild cenſure, and your
ſelfe to your ſoules
content.

Yours in deſire

Ioh: Weeuer.

A2b, A3a

In commendation of the worke and the
Author.

Nor doſt thou praiſe,a pockworne tawnie trull,
Nor doſt thou carue a liueleſſe ſlubbred ſtone,
Nor doſt thou fill thy page with great othes full,
Nor doſt thou ſonnet of King Salomon:
Nor doſt thou like a loue-ſicke milke-ſop gull,
Vnto thy Miſtris for a kiſſe make mone:
But ſalt with ſugar,honnie mixt with gall,
Muſt needes be praiſde,muſt needes be likt of al.

Now I am ſure thou tendes to vertues lore,
Shewes reading,iudgement,and inuention,
Thus writ the Epigrammatiſts of yore,
And told the world her foule abuſion:
    Thus thou and thine ſhal euer enui de be,
    And like a Page will Enuy tend on thee.

A 3   Why

In Authorem.

Why so? *Alcyon* maketh first her nest,
And then into the riuer lets it slide,
To see if t'wil keepe water from her brest;
So thou thy nest my friend in me hast tride:
  I like it wel, it holdeth water out,
  Feare sier, sier is the curious scout.

        T.B.Gen.

In Authorem.

I wish my rough-hewne lines might gratifie,
The first borne of thy pleasing Poesie,
These be but blossomes: what will be the fruite,
When time and age, hath made thee more acute?
Meane while how euer *Momus* bite the lippe,
Each man will praise the weauers workmanship:
When wittie verse is worthily regarded,
Then shall thy verse be thankfully rewarded.

        I.K.Mag: Art.

So

Ad Librum.

So great a sence withing in so short a verse,
So great a worke within so short a space,
So great aduise to find in so few yeares,
Addes fame to *Grant*, and thee to Muses race.

These Epigrams the buds of thy first spring,
Shew what thy leaues in summer time will be,
For more they do sprout forth, the more thou sing
That th'after age thy wit may verifie,
  Thus *Grant* is made *Pyrene* our willowes baies
  This Booke the honor of thy yong wise daies.

    Tho: Kedgewin Gent. Vincit qui patitur.

A 4   Of

To the Author.

Of Hemp and wooll our country weauers make,
Such kind of cloth as keeps vs whole and cleane,
This silken *Weeuer* subtler loomes gin take,
And seu'n weeks web hath warpt with finer beam,
  His cloth discouereth vice,
    adorning vertues lore,
  Wherefore of greater price,
    then Weauers heretofore.

        Ed: Gurney. Gent.

In laudem Authoris.

Αἶς τὸ λοξὶα τὸν ψιθύρισμον ἀκήειν,
Ο᾽ρχης τε Διὸς παιγνίμονας τε θὲας,
Ο᾽υ γὰρ λόγον ὅτος ἔλκυσε λινέργον Α᾽δηπι:
Η᾽δ᾽ιον ὀυκ Ε᾽γμῖς παιδ᾽ρὸς ἐγεύτε μελὸς
Ποικίλον ὀυν ἔργον, πολυδ᾽αίδαλα γράμματα ταῦλα
Κιδ᾽ος ἔχει φανερὸν κ᾽ ἄπαῦ᾽ον ἄθλον ἔχει.

        Quaris

Eiusdem.
In laudem Authoris

Quaris Amalthea cornu? mem quaris & Artis?
Nec sine mente iocos? & sine dente sales?
Huc vertes osculos, animumq̃, aduerte benignum,
Praclarum docta respice mentis opus,
Sape Poeta nouem, celebrauit carmine musas?
Nunc decima audita est, carmina Musa loqui.
      M. Milward mag: Ar:
      Statuto bono , sta tuto

Lectores, quotquot, quales, quicunq̃, estis.

O let my words be sweetned in a mouth,
(If your great highnesse can discend so low,
As daigne to view my tender-blush-ing youth,
That twenty twelue months yet did neuer know)
Right *Malmsey* relisht: one which euer saith,
Good, very good, nay, excellent in faith.

Dew

I]ew gracious lookes vpon mine infant Muse,
Nip not my blossoms in their budding prime,
These artlesse lines at leisure do peruse,
Only to adde more wings to idle time:
If thou ring muse could neuer get that spirit,
Which to peruse me might your fauour merit.

I neuer lay vpon a bed of Roses,
Twixt Beauties lips entombing of my tong,
Smelling rose-waterd odoriferous Poses,
Pleasing my mistris with a Mermaides song.
Of amorous kissing more then loue-sicke lauish,
Whose iuice might make my words the Readers
(rauish.

The liquid waues nor did I euer plash
Of siluer-channeld *Ysis* purling riuer,
(Yet *Vestor*-old nymph-nursing *Grant* wil wash
Hir Nymphs: & scorns preheminēce to giue hir)
Nor haue I spent in *Troinouant* my dayes,(Bayes.
Where all good witts(some say)are crown d with
                                                             I

I cannot shew then in a sugred vaine,
Wit,iudgement,learning,or inuention:
I cannot reach vp to a *Delians* straine,
Whose songs deserue for euer your attention:
Nor *Draytons* stile,whose hony words are meete
For these your mouths,far more than hony sweet.

I neuer durst presume take in mine hand
The nimble-tripping Faëries history,
I cannot,I protest,yet vnderstand
The wittie,learned, Satyres mystery;
I cannot moue the sauage with delight,
Of what I cannot, Reader then I write.

Must I then cast in Enuies teeth defiance?
Or dedicate my Poems to detraction?
Or must I scorne *Castilioe's* neere alliance?
Nay,I must praise this Poet-pleasing faction;
Lest in the Presse my ouerthrow they threaten;
And of the Binders laugh to see me beaten.   O

O that I had such eloquence as might
Intreate the enuious Reader boue the rest,
(For his deepe wisedome censures all aright)
That by his lippes I may be alwaies blest!
If this suffice not for the enuiest,
Know then, I am an Epigrammatist.
                        John Weeuer.

Intentio operis & Authoris.

For pride with *Clio Tamyras* contend,
For profit *Otho,*all thy Poems spend,
Pedro for praise,praise *Burdineroes* vice,
Please thou thy selfe,in reading ouer thrice
Tubro thy verse.Speake faire ye Gnatonists,
But whip and scourge ye Epigrammatists:
To whip and scourge,my chiefest meaning is,
With seu'n sower rods laid ful seu'n weeks in pisse
Yet pleasure,profit,pride,nor praise allures me,
To whip & scurge. But vertue that procures me.
                        To

To the generous Readers.

Pigramms are much like vnto Almanacks seruing especially for the yeare for the which they are made, then these (right iudging Readers)being for one yeare pend, and in another printed: are past date before they come from the Presse, that you may put them vp in your pockets(like your old Almanacks) as not befiting this triumphant yeere of Iubile:yet I beseech you shew me some curtesie,in hope to haue the next calculated more carefully. If you looke for some reasons because I keep no order in the placing of my Epistles and Epigrams, let this suffice, I write Epigrams, and there is an old saying:
    Non locus hominem,sed homo locum, &c:
            —*The placing giues no grace*
    Vnto the man,but man vnto the place.
    Some faultes you shall finde in the printing, and more in the penning, all which I referre to your owne correction, and my selfe to your mild censures.

                        Ioh: Weeuer.

Epig. 1. De se.

NOr do I feare the Satyres venim'd bite,
  Nor choplogs teeth, ne Railors vile reproch,
Nor male-contented Enuies poysned spight,
Ioues thunderbolt, nor *Momus* long sharp broch.
Nor that I haue in high *Parnassus* slept,
Or pledg'd *Apollo* Cups of Massicke wine:
Or by the fount of *Helicon* haue kept,
That none dare carp these Epigrammes of mine;
  But that I thinke I shall be carpt of none,
  For who'le wrest water from a flintie stone?

Epig. 2. Ad Lectorem

Of all my Epigrams, Reader, reade not one,
Ne yet reade two, but rather reade iust none;
Then reade them all, or let them all alene.

B   7

Epig. 3. In Elizabetham.

If that *Elizium* be no fained thing,
Whereof the Poëts wont so much to sing;
Then are those faire fields in this Faërie land,
Which faire *Eliza* rules with awfull hand:
By BAI th' Ægyptians signifie the soule,
Which doth the bodies appetites controule,
ETH signifies mans hart, from whence we know
The fountaine of their vitall breath doth flow.
ELIZA giues this land the name: BAI soule; hart ETH
Name, soul, hart, of this land ELIZABETH.

Epig. 4. In Cormungum.

Cormung did wish wel alwaies to the poore,
Wishing they had of Corne or money store:
When wishing would not fill the poor mans box
The poore man wisht, and *Cormung* had the pox.

Thou'rt

Epig. 5. In Crassum.

Thou'rt medling with my hat, and medling with (my shoos,
Thou'rt medling with my ruffes, and medling
    with my hose:
Thou'rt medling with my gate, and medling with
    my lookes,
Thou'rt medling with my wit, and medling with
    my bookes:
Crassus, thy medling hath this guerdon only gottē
Medlers are neuer ripe before that they be rotten.

Epig. 6. In Brillum.

Two Contraries more glorious farre appeare,
When each to other they be placed neare:
Vntil I knew this axiom I did muse,
Why Gentlemen so much do Bases vse:
Yet *Brillus* Bases addes to *Brill* no grace,
But make him baser, whom by birth is base:
  Gentilitie then *Brillus* first should get,
  Before base *Brillus* do in Bases iet.

B 2   My

Epig.7. De Epigr. suis.

My Epigrams were all new ready made,
And onely on the Printers leisure staid;
One of my friends on Sheeps greene I did meet,
Which to'd me one was printing in Bridge street:
And would(if so it pleasde to come thither)
Print with a warrant both gainst wind & wether.
I thanked him:my Booke to Presse now goes:
But I am gulld,he printeth onely hose.

Epig.8. In Thyrum.

Thyrus,thou told'st one I might be asham'd
To print these papers;and it did sore greeue thee,
And that thou wouldst in print be neuer nam'd:
Thou dar'st not Thyrus therefore I beleeue thee;
Yet twixt vs two this strife we may soone stint
Looke at your breeches,are they not in print?

Witte

Epig.9. De Ingenio, Fortuna, Fama.

Witte scorned Fortune,followed after Fame,
That throgh the world she might extol his name;
Fortune scorned Wit,and gaue him this therfore,
He might haue Fame,but euer with it poore.

Epig.10. De Fama, & Amore.

Flie thou from Loue,and it wil follow thee
But folow Fame,and it wil flie from thee:
Then flie from Fame,and follow Loue,if either;
Then thou'lt loose fame,& yet attain loue neither:
Since diuers are the waies of Loue and Fame,
No maruel then thogh loue oft end with shame.

B 3   Boscus

Epig.11. In Boscum.

Boscus at boules his shoulders cannot want,
He thinkes belike thei're made of Adamant:
What way he would his brasil bowle should wed
That way he doth alwayes his shoulders bend:
Hob,hob he cries,pox on that hob,naght's good,
Blow wind,hold Byas,succour there,Gods ( )
But Byas wrong,that oth not shoulders drew it
Iust by an asse,backe to the asse which threw it.

Epig.12. De carne leporina.

Phni reports of all beasts in their kind,
The flesh is best of a swift footed hare:
It doth not onely beautifie the mind,
But makes the bodie,face,surpassing faire:
I wonder then why connies in request
Shuld so much be,when hares flesh is the best.

It's

Epig.13. In Rogerum Manners Rut-landiæ Comitem.

It's not the sea which doth our land inclose,
That makes vs mightie to withstand our foes:
Nor farmes,nor mannours,but where manners be
There stands the cittie,from foes danger free;
If Manners then make vs our foes withstand,
MANNERS may wel be cald ROOT of the LAND.

Epig.14. In Crassum.

Crassus will say the dogge faunes with his taile,
To men of worth he writes for's best auaile:
Crassus thou lyest, dogs write not deedes of men,
Then thou the dog that snarlest at my pen.

B 4   Mono-

Epig.15. In Monocerotem.

Monoceros hath ſtrength,but hath no witte,
And therefore one horne will the foole befitte:
But how can't be that he but one horne haue?
When to his neighbour Bruſus two he gaue?

Epig.16. De Pœno.

Poore Pœnus had ſince ſtatute was made ſo,
At eu'ry towne ſome cheare,but whip and go:
But euer ſince the Clari-cords came in,
Of whipping cheare he ſurfeited had bin:
He neuer thankes his deereſt friends therefore,
That ſuch good cheere prouided for the poore;
Except the Conſtables were phiſitians good,
To know the ſigne before they let him bloud.

Felix

Epig.17. In Felicem.

Felix the foole,I ſaid,as fooliſh writte,
Therein my ſelfe more fooliſh I did ſhow,
But then he prou'd himſelfe to haue no witte,
That did not call me aſſe for ſaying ſo.

Epig. 18.

Aske Lygdus who a Poet is by right,
He with harſh Horace thus will anſwere ſtraight,
He that hath pulld his haire quite from his beard,
And can inuent braue oths wold make one feard,
Pulld off his nailes,and left no haire on's head,
Thus would he haue himſelfe a Poet read;
For Lygdus had a waſhing for three pence
Three yeares ago, he ne're need ſhauing ſince.

If

Epig. 19 In Nigellum

IfI ſhould chooſe,yea,for my life,
To be thy hawke (Nigell) or wife,
I would the hawke chuſe of the one,
She weares a hood,thy wife weares none.

Epig.20 In eundem

Dogs thou doſt loue, dogs thou doſt feede,
Thy wife thou hat'ſt in time of neede;
And ſtill with her thou art at ſtrife,
Better to be thy dog than wife.

Evig. 21

One ſued for ſeruice at Florellaes ſhrine;
Florella kindly did him entertaine
To be her ſeruant,ſhe a Saint diuine;
This high preferment glad he was to gaine;
To make this match her frends he forward foūd,
If but this one thing he himſelfe would grant,
To feoffe her by yeare in forty pound:
He tried his wit (for wit oft comes by want)
And brought them ſtrait within his ſtudie doore,
And there he ſhew'd them old Orations,
A common place-booke of ten quire and more,
Latines,Verſes,Theames and Declamations;
He ſwore theſe coſt four hundred pound at leaſt,
(May be at learning he had ſpent ſo much)
Thats fortie pound a yeare by intereſt.
But marke,her friends ſeru'd him a craftie tuch,
You ſhal haue her (ſay they)but firſt know well,
For ſo much coine you muſt your papers ſell.

Some

The firſt weeke.

Epig.22 De ſe.

Some men marriage doe commend,
And all their life in wiuing ſpend;
But if that I ſhould wiues haue three,
(God keepe me from Polygamie)
   Ile giue the diuell two for pay,
   If he will fetch the third away.

Epig 23 Ad Michaelem Drayton.

The Peeres of heau'n kept a parliament,
And for Wittes-mirrour Philip Sidney ſent,
To keepe another when they doe intend,
Twentie to one for Drayton they will ſend,
   Yet bade him leaue his learning,ſo it fled,
   And vow'd to liue with thee ſince he was dead

Finis.

To the right worſhipfull and no-
ble minded Gentleman, Robert
Dalton of Pilling
Eſquier.

Earing (right Worſhipfull) leſt I ſhould die altogether vngratefull, Occaſion euery day proffers herſelfe to performe more than my wit dare preſume to promiſe : and it will be long (I feare me) before they iumpe in a full point. In the meane time, take (I beſeech you) a few lines in this waſte peece of paper , in part of a Schollers payment. And withall,if not a Gerfalcon, thinke yet I ſend you a Hawke, which will be agreeable to my wiſh, and your Worſhips worthineſſe.

Ioh: Weeuer.

B6b, B7a

The ſecond weeke.

Epig.I Ad Robertum Dalton Armig.

GRace thou(kind Dalton)with a ſmiling looke,
Theſe rude pend lines of this my ſecōd book;
And I,my Muſe, and Graces three wil praiſe
Thy iudgement,wit,and valour:
But I, my Muſe,and Graces, are too few,
To pen thy praiſe, to whom al praiſe is due.

Epig 2 In Tortonem

Torto hath croſt his ierkin and his hoſe,
So without croſſes Torto neuer goes,
(Except whenas he dallies with his whore,
For then croſt Torto runnes vpon the ſcore;
By all good tokens Roll a kiſſing tooke:
And Item for, did ſet on Tortoes booke)
   His greateſt croſſe, that wil croſſe al,I dread,
   Is,he wants croſſes for to croſſe his head.

when

B7b, B8a

Epig.3 In Titum

When hare-brain'd Titus.

Desunt nonnulla.

Epig.

Epig.4.

When witte is waining thus we write of want,
As though our workes were all lost by the way:
Or for their goodnesse stolne were we vaunt,
And printed sore against our wills we say;
   Lets write in want, for I haue tried this,
   Than one too many, want one better is.

Epig.5.   De nomine in Marmore sculpto.

Great Marcus made his pure proud marble toom
In Pauls Church wall, for lacke of better roome:
Foule snake-ei d Enuy, s'daining his great praise,
Hath cut M.thus(i i)as thogh she meant to raze
His name quite forth of Fames immortal booke,
And breakes the stones, makes all vnseemly looke:
   If stones and names decay, what wonder then
   Thogh death destroy vs weak and mortal men?

C   Ruffinus

Epig.6.   In Ruffinum.

Ruffinus lost his tongue on stage,
And wot ye how he made it knowne?
He spittes it out in bloudy rage,
And told the people he had none:
   The fond spectators said, he acted wrong,
   The dumbest man may say, he hath no tongue.

Epig 7.   In eundem.

Ruffinus hath no tongue, why?
   For now he lost one:
Ruffinus hath a tongue, why?
   He saies he hath none.

Cario

Epig.8.   De Carione.

Cario bragges and sweares his wife's a maide,
A louely Lucrece, or Diana rather:
Some sacred Sant in womans clothes arraide,
And why? his children are so like their father:
   Yet Carioe's cousoned, do what e're he can,
   She thinks of him, lies with another man.

Epig.9.   In Coruum.

Now old-cook Coruus you which do yet scorn it,
That your faire Fulna with her golden haire
Should rub your head, & afterwards then horn it,
And al because you see no hornes appeare:
But in thy mouth another man more seeth, (teeth.
In faith thou'rt horned : thou want'st thine vpper

C 2   Nihil

Epig. 10.

—————— Nihil hic nisi carmina desunt:
—————— Nihil hic nisi berbera desunt:
fire yp but 20 yfd all, friend?

Epig. 11. In D.D. Palmer.

Palmers in woods liu'd onely by the Palme,
And gaue to paffengers the fweeteft balme:
In wilderneffe when any went aftray,
Then Palmers fet them in the ready way:
So Palmer liues by our frefh Palme the Queene,
(Victorious Palme-tree grow thou euer greene:)
And in a wood or wilderneffe doth tell
The paffengers which way they may goe well:
(For the world is a wilderneffe of woe,
Like paffengers the people in it goe:)
  Thus Palmer liues and giues the fweeteft balm,
  To Palmer then of right belongs the palme.

Palmers

C 3   Caftilio

Epig. 12. In Caftilionem malum quendam Poetam.

Caftilio writes when he might hold his tongue,
Caftilio craues, though pardon for his writing,
That's to confeffe vnto the world his wrong:
Which of the world (at leaft) deferue's endiuing:
  Well, thus the world is guilty of his fin, (him?
  And the world hangs, how can the world hang

Epig. 13. In eundem.

Caftilioe's ficke vpon it,
  Ioue help him in his anguifh,
Left that worfe verfe he vomit,
  So oft as he doth languifh.

A

Epig. 14. Ad Philerotem.

A great demeane friend Phileros you haue,
And feuen wiues all lying in their graue:
But yet the churchyard farre more profit yeelds,
Than all the reuenewes of your faireft fields.

Epig. 15. In Stratum.

Fortie foure pence brought Stratus to a play,
Fortie foure pounds he carried yet away:
A Coni-catcher who calls him for the fame?
A Money-catcher may be Stratus naine.

C 4   How

Epig. 16. In obitum piissimi, sapientissimi, omniq́; virtutum genere cumulatissimi viri Richardi Vpcheri Armig.

How Nature triumph't at this *Vpchers* birth!
Swore he should be th'ornament of the earth:
In him she placed her imperiall throne,
As though mankind remaind in him alone:
All Wisedome, Vertue, Courage in his brest,
As in their fairest lodge should alwaies rest:
But when Death saw this better worke of Nature,
And all perfections found in this one creature;
Death likewise triumph't, and was wondrous glad
That such a Champion to assault he had:
  Whom if he kill'd he kill'd (he kild we find)
  All Wisdome, Vertue, Courage, and Mankind.

Some

Epig. 17. In Caluum.

Some say that *Caluus* lately lost his haire,
By *Paris* garden bayting a white beare,
The wiser sort affirme that he was shauen
In Deuils ditch, Knaues acre, Cuckolds hauen:
  Aske *Caluus*, he of scripture makes a scorne,
  Naked hee le die, for naked he was borne.

Epig. 18. In obitum Mirmedontis,

Here lies the man who whilom in a trance
At *Tiburne* di'de wounded by men of *France*,
For wading *Tiburne* there he got a quease,
Which brought the perpendicular disease,
And afterward of rope-seede tooke a surfet,
Which causd him be canuast in a hempon bläket;
  Well, *Mirmedon* was sure to go to wrecke,
  When that red headed *Taurus* rulde the necke

Epig.

Epig. 19. In Lollus.

The lurcher *Lollus* at the Ordinarie,
Wisest of all mens manners in the Cittie,
Another sot applaudes him sitting by
Thus: Sir, by heau'ns, that was wondrous wittie:
  I ouer-heard, and when I heard the best,
  In faith t'was but an ordinarie iest.

Epig. 20. In eundem.

I laugh't aloude to heare this wind-falne man
Say, that he courted (at the play) his whore;
Shall Court run currant for a Curtezan?
Were Ladies euer thus abusde before?
  Then *Ioue* a boone yeeld, yeeld to my request,
  Make me a Ladie, for his sake at least.

Epig.

Epig. 21. In obitum sepulcrum Gullionis.

Here lies fat *Gullio*, who caperd in a cord
To highest heau'n for all his huge great weight,
His friends left at *Tiburne* in the yere of our Lord
  1   5   9   and   8
What part of his body French men did not eate,
That part he giues freely to worms for their meat

Epig. 22. In Coam.

A nor Ω will *Coa* espie,
Till she ascend vp to the corner'd Π.

Epig.

The second weeke.

Epig. 23 _Ad Robertum Dalton Armig._

Kindnes it felfe,and Vertues vicegerent,
Learnings maintainer, Pouerties releeuer,
Valours bright enfigne, Honors heire apparent,
Gentlemans behauiour,Governments vpholder,
Thefe titls claim,thefe,more thē thefe thine own,
If more may be,or more in mā was known.

Epig. 24 _In Vertumnum iudicem._

Wicked _Vertumnus_ _Perylus_ redeem'de,
With (τ) though (Θ) _Perilus_ deferu'de,
For _Chion_ (Θ) though it better feem'de
For _Chion_ (τ) for _Chion_ neuer fweru'de:
With (Λ) _Lolus_ held in law too long,
Thus _Peril,Chion,Lolus_ he did wrong.

Epig.

The second weeke.

Epig. 25 _Ad Lectorem_

Curteous kind Reader,find my meaning out,
Whilft that I go the hemifphære about,
My wit's in waining,darke,obfcure,and dull,
Therefore muft change before it be at full:
To _Phœbus_ orbe my wit doth goe this night,
Of him to borrow fome tranfpiercing light.

Finis.

To the right wor_fhipfull_, _fir Ri_-chard Mallineux knight, indued with the depth of wifedome, and all good gouernement.

He wifeft Romans(right Worfhipfull) de-lighted in the counterfet geftures of Rof-cius; the graueft Cato would haue his fe-ftiual day to frolicke in: then I thinke your thoughts intended to moft ferious ftudies, will fome-times take delight in trifles. _And for a preparatiue to your mind-refrefhing paftime, here are a few pilles, which will purge melancholy: Prouided alwayes this, that litle is their vertue in operation, vnleffe you par-don the giuers prefumption._

Ioh: Weeuer.

Epig. I *De Interlunio,*

The half fac'd *Moone* nights gouernesse did chãg
When in the Crab the Sunne was retrograde;
To th'hot dry Lion strait she meant to range,
Till with the Dog in longitude he staide:
So this next week by these signes you may gather
You must expect crab'd,dry and dogged wether

*Epig.*2 *In Fuscam*

Tell me *Bollana* if thou can,
What meanes thy Mistris weare a fan?
So faire a fan, so fowle a face,
*Fusca,*or fan,must needes disgrace.

D   Wise

*Epig.*3 *Ad D. Mounteagle.*

*Mounteagle,*which art now thy cuntries pride,
Vnto thy worth would I could tune my verse,
Then Wit and Art,and all I would prouide,
To be thy Poet,and thy praise rehearse:
    But with my Art I cannot equall thee,   (me.
    Then thou thy self must needes commend for

*Epig.*4 *De homine in Luna.*

When *Bunas* view'd the wandring plannets seau'n
He spide a knaue in Moone all cloth'd in blacke,
Who for his theft could come no nearer heau'n,
But bore a bush of sharp thornes on his backe:
    A knaue in Moone?what neede he look so hie?
    When in the Sunne a thousand stoode him by.

Wisdomes

*Epig.*5 *In Ramistas.*

Wisedomes adopted heire say what thou can,
Ramists defend in Moone to be a man,
If please him pisse,then he doth send vs raine,
If drunke,a deluge,and a watry maine: (yeere,
Come down thou man since *Sturbridge* fair foure
Thy pissing made vs all drinke single beere.

*Epig.*6. *In eosdem.*

Frõ whence doth come this root-vpriuing wind?
From the moons man,when he doth blow behind
Snow,frost,and haile,be scales in's hoary crown,
And from his nose the mildew drops ydowne:
His Camphire breath doth all perfume the aire,
Bedews the flowers,& makes the fields seem fair:
Vapours arising from the earth his meate,
And like a glutton he doth alwaies eate:
I thinke those men be wiser farre then these,
Who think the moon is made all of green cheese.

D 2   Hence

The third weeke.

Epig. 7. Ad fatorum dominum

Hence *Braurens* god to *Taurominion*,
And you leualting *Corybants* be gone,
Fly thundering *Bronsterops* to *Hyppocrene*,
And *Mauors* to Nymph-nursing *Mytilene*,
Griefly *Megaeraes* necromanticke spell
Depart to blacke nights Acheronticke Cell,
Avaunt transformed *Epidaurian*,
Vnto th'Antipod Isles of *Taproban:*
Away *Cyllenius* plume-pinion'd god,
With thy peace-making wand, snake-charming
And al the rest, not daring looke vpon   (rod,
Vranus blood-borne brood and fell *Typhon*,
Chymaraes victor great *Bellerephon*,
Thou vanquisher of Spanish *Geryon*,
Stowt *Hadruball Sicilian* Lord of yore,
Thou that destroyd'st the *Calidonian* Bore
Couragious Conqueror of *Creetes Minotaure*,

Thou

The third weeke.

Thou pride of *Mermeros* cloudy *Semitaure*,
Perseus, whose marbl-stone-transforming shield
Enforc'd the whale *Andromeda* vp yeeld,
You *Argonautes* that scowr'd *Syndromades*,
And pass'd the quicke-sands of *Symplegades*.
Help *Demogorgon* king of heau'n and earth,
Cheo's Lucina at *Litigium's* birth:
The world with child lookes for deliuerie,
Of Canniballs or *Poetophagie*,
A diuelish broode from *Erichthonius*,
From *Iphidemia, Nox* and *Erebus*,
Chide *Pegasus* for op'ning *Helicon*,
And Poets damne to *Pyrithlegeton*,
Or make this monstrous birth abortiue be,
Or else I will shake hands with Poetrie.

D 3   Say

The third weeke.

Epig. 8 Ad Lectorem.

Say you that I am obscure?
Why this is yong mens Rhetoricke,
Owles must not iudge of *Coruus* sure,
For he speakes nought but Rhetoricke:
    Either too high, or els too plaine,
    And this is now a schollers vaine.

Epig. 9 In Battum.

Battus affirm'd no Poet euer writte,
Before that Loue inspir'd his dull head witte,
And yet himselfe in Loue had witte no more,
Than one stark mad, thogh somwhat wise before.

Os

The third weeke.

Epig 10. De Ore.

Os of *O*, a mouth *Scaliger* doth make,
And from this letter, mouth his name doth take:
I had beene in *Scalligers* beleefe,
But that I lookt in *O*, and saw no teeth.

Epig 11 In Fuscam.

Is *Fuscaes* fan gainst winter, wind, and sunne?
She scornes their force so bright her face is done:
Is *Fuscaes* fan to flap away the flies,
Dare they come nere her eagle-sighted eies?
    Belike they thinke she is some Butchers shop,
    Her face the flesh whereon they vse to lop.

D 4   Is

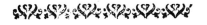

Epig. 12 In Byrrham

Is *Byrrha* browne? who doth the question aske?
Her face is pure as Ebonie teat blacke,
It's hard to know her face from her faire maske,
Beautie in her seemes beautie still to lacke.
Nay, shee's snow-white, but for that russet skin,
Which like a vaile doth keep her whitenes in.

Epig. 13 In Roderingonem

If Beard can make a good Diuine,
  Then *Rodering* is one:
But Beard can make no good Diuine,
  Then *Rodering* is none.

Where

Epig. 14 In eundem

Where Iuie-bush hangs out say I,
There you may wine for money buy:
Yet he for all his bushie signe,
Is but a grapelesse dead drie vine:
  For take his beard from off his chin,
  Both bare without, and bare within.

Epig. 15 In Fucam

In *Fucaes* face the Graces seeme to mart,
So like she is the blushing rose-red morne,
Sure in her shape the Gods all bore a part,
A withered Hermite fiue-score winters worne
Might shake off fiftie, seeing her beforne:
  Yet *Fura* dare not venture in the ayre,
  For feare the water wash away her fayre.

First

Epig. 16 In obitum Gloriani.

First life, then death, next death was life before,
And death gaue life, a life for euermore:
Life was not life, til death gaue life, life better,
To death for life then *Glorian* is a debter.

Epig. 17 In Lycum pædagogum

Many are beholding *Lycus* for thy paine,
Which with their sons and daughters thou hast
Beleeue me *Lycus*, I did often wonder   (taine:
To see the wenches proue so well you vnder:
If that but once to Learnings lore you win them
This I dare sweare, you can put learning in them.

Daphne

Epig. 18 De Daphnide Apollinem fugiente.

Daphne of *Apollo* neuer was afraid,
But of the weapons which *Apollo* had;
So modest maides of men stand not in feare,
But of the weapons which we men do beare.

Epig. 19 In Brutum

The gallant *Brutus* iettes it in the streets,
Faine would haue all looke at his face he meetes.
And lest he passe vnseene this way doth find,
To cut his shooes before broad, and behind
He puts in quills, as if his shooes would say,
(Stand passengers and view me in your way)
And yet the foole what he wold haue doth loose
For none looke at his face, all at his shooes.

Sabidi

D4b, D5a

D5b, D6a

Epig.20 Tranflat. ex Martial.

Sabidi I loue thee not,nor why I wot,
But this I wot,*Sabidi* I loue thee not.

Epig.21 De Georgio Graue non fepulto.

Graue was *George Graue*,his grauenes caufd him
(die,
Graue fhuld to graue,yet *Graue* doth graueles lie.

Epig.22 In Gulielmum Couel.

Couel thy mind thou haft already feafon'd,
With falt of wit, and relifh of all Artes,
With *Plato* oft,and *Aristotle* reafon d,
Seeking all meanes to beautifie all partes,
That twixt thy lips diuinitie doth fall,
Like Berill drops from fome faire criftall wall.

Sad

Epig.23 In D.D. Ouerall Reg.profeff.

Sad Sifters futed in defpairing blacke,
Curbe Cares vnreft,fing Carolles now againe,
Leane rake-tooth'd Death is like to go to wracke,
Of *Whitaker* a *Phœnix* breedes againe:
One ouer Death,moreouer,ouer More,
One ouer you, nay yet one ouer all.
Deaths ouerthrow let *Ouerall* be therefore,
A Victors praife of you deferue he fhall.
And if my pen could *Ouerall* giue breath,
Then *Ouerall* fhould ftill be ouer death.

Finis.

when

To the right worfhipfull, fir Ed-
ward Warren knight, graced with al
giftes both of the minde
and bodie.

I Doe prefume(right Wor:)to offer vp to
your good liking thefe fmall indeuours far
vnworthy the looking ouer of your fo worthy felfe,yet becaufe I am altogether de-
ftitute of a better prefent, I hope this fmall performance will be as willingly accepted, as zealoufly offered, and (hereafter) I vow thus to deuide my chiefeft
ftudies,one part of the day fhalbe denoted to your Wor-
fhips remembrance,and another of the night, in wifh-
ing you all health and happineffe.

Ioh: Weeuer.

*Epig.1 Ad anunculum fuum Henricum
Butler Armig.*

IF From the conqueft thy antiquitie
I would deriue, when *William* gaue thy mot,
Or boaft the *Butlers* true gentiltie,
My praifes yet augment thy praife would not.
Nay praife would be difpraife thy name to blot,
Ne will I praife;or praife thy felfe alone,
Or good deedes praife,or praifes looke for none.

Epig.2 In Daconem

The Diuel and *Dacon* both by chance did meete,
With congies faire either did other greete,
The Diuel would dice,but *Dacon* had no crowns
Dacon his foule pledg'd for a thoufand pounds;
Dacon could cogge,and fo the Diuell paid
His thoufand pounds, a thoufand more yet had:
Is cogging then I pray you fuch an euil?
Nay, ti s a quiddit how to cheate the Deuill.

Epig.

Epig. 3 In obitum fortiſſimi ducis Io: Vpcheri.
Sound a retrait, ye common ſouldiers ſound,
When captains thus imperious death dare woûd,
And ſteale to ſteele in powders ſmoalue maske,
Where Valour lockt was in his plumed caske:
Nay, ſpite of Death (like him) yet weeping come,
And ſet this Verſe on his heroicke Tombe:
  Here Vpcher lies, who ſtriuing Death reſiſt,
  Di'de with the fawchon in his manly fiſt.

Epigramma
The wiſe Gramarian reprehends my Muſe,
Which *In* for praiſefull Epigrams doth vſe
This Rule; *In pro erga, contra & ad,*
Will proue your good wiſe gramariſme bad.

Epi. 4 Ad R o: Allot, & Chr. Middleton.
Quicke are your wits, ſharp your conceits,
  Short, and more ſweete your layes:
Quicke, but no wit, ſharpe, no conceit,
  Short, and leſſe ſweete, my praiſe.
                                    Fame

Epig. 5 In Thomam Oxburghe
Fame loſt ſome feathers, yet I imp t hir plumes,
My needle naught, Fame ſlies, but yet the tunes,
Becauſe ſhe can thy praiſes not vpreare,
Nor with the Falcon fetch a cancelleere.
  Why thus it is when Falc'ners haue no s' ill,
  And yet will ſhew a Falconers good wil.

Epig. 6 In Hypocritam fabrum.
I told thee *Sutor Faber* was a ſtarre,
And that he ſhined bright aboue compare:
But ſince he went into the Spaniſh warre,
A rapier for a Bible he doth weare:
The Spaniſh Cut graceth his holy face,
His friend he croſſes with a conge or cringe,
His wiſes gowne's laid thicke with veluet lace,
Her petticorte is furr'd with coſtly fringe:
  So falne he is, but Stars vſe not to fall,
  He was a Comet, and deceiu'd vs all.
                                    E   A

Epig. 7 In Bunnam.
A ſhaue-beard Barber *Bunna* chanc'd to meete,
As ſhe was going all along the ſtreete;
The Barber ſweares hee's glad they met ſo right,
She ſhould barb him, or he barb her that night:
What was the reaſon of this their debate?
Or what's the cauſe why Barbers *Bunna* hate?
Bunna, ſhe barbs too cheap, and barbs by'th ſcore
And whom ſhe barbes they ne're neede barbing
                                    (more.

Epig. 8. De Palmone.
Palmo, a Poet, Goldſmith, or a Glouer,
That ſo with gloues *Nans* loue thou doſt retaine;
A thouſand verſes of a faithfull louer
Could not ſuffice, but thou muſt ſend a chaine:
Nan laugh's at thee, and wiſheth in her heart,
The chaine were longer, and the letter ſhort.
                                    Eripha

Epig. 9 In Eripham vetulam.
Eripha that old trot euery day
Waits o're the water for to ſee a play,
And there a withered ore-worne face ſhe ſhows
Beſet with Rubies, and ſtopt full of Oos.
This water-witch a patch hath for th'rheume,
Her carkas ſhe with Aloes doth perfume;
With muske, ciuit, olibane, myrrh, incenſe,
Breathing out an aromaticke redolence:
Her foulneſſe makes me oft mine eies vp cloſe,
Her ſweetnes makes me wiſh I were all Noſe.

Epig. 10 In Steronem Legiſlatorem.
Nor do I praiſe thy heart, thats ill intending,
Nor yet thy mouth thats fooliſh and a lier,
Nor yet thine eies, thei're purblind ſtil offending,
Nor thy falſe teng, that is a burning fier,
Nor hands, for hands take oft more than their fees
Nor arms, nor legs, nor breſt, nor back, nor knees
                                    E 2   Yet

Yet *Steron* giue me but one weeke thy vailes,
And I will praife, thy haire, thy beard, thy nailes.

Epig. II   *In Spurium quendam fcriptorem.*

Apelles did fo paint faire *Venus* Queene,
That moft fuppofde he had faire *Venus* feene,
But thy bald rimes of *Venus* fauour fo,
That I dare fweare thou doft all *Venus* know.

Epig. 12   *In Hugonem.*

Though praife and pleafe doth *Hugo* neuer none
Yet praife and pleafe doth *Hugo* euer one,
For praife and pleafe doth *Hugo* himfelfe alone.

was't

Epig. 13   *In D.D.Plaifer.*

Was't heauenly *Plato* in whofe mouth they fay
The Bees were wont their honie combs to lay;
From whofe fweet lips fo fweet a found did flow,
As neuer *Orpheus* made in hell below?
Mellifluous Plaifer, fo men call thy name,
And why *Mellifluous* but for *Platoes* fame?
Thy heauenly Muficke notes charming fo well,
Can fetch mans foule faire *Euridice* from hell.
  Since *Orpheus* Harp thou haft, & *Platoes* Bee,
Mellifluous Plaifer, fitteft name for thee.

F 3   *Matho*

Epig 14.   *Ad Mathonem.*

Matho I'm told that many do thinke much,
Becaufe I call you Piller of the Church:
Matho, you bought a Deanry at belt rate,
And two church-liuings now impropriate,
And fold to *Gnidus* a rich Parfonage;
(For diuers caufes) gaue a Vicarage:
And now hath got three liuings at one lurch:
Art thou not then a pillar of the Church?

Epig. 15   *In obitum Roberti Shute Iufl.de Reg.Banco.*

Shute did ere-while the Country fofter,
No peny now, no *pater nofter*,
O defperate Death, how could'ft thou dare,
To put our Country thus to care?

Could

Could not his Iuftice fet him free?
Nor yet his Law perfwade with thee?
Could not his honour ftay the fire,
Which was the credite of the fhire?
When Death fuch Lawyers doth out-face,
Then punies may not pleade the cafe.
When Captaine once doth fall on ground,
Then Souldiers the retaite may found:
If Peeres to ground do goe fo faft,
Let pefants know they muft at laft.
A fhoote was fhot which loft the game,
And yet the *Shute* hath wonne the fame.
The fhoote was fhot vp very high,
Which from the earth to heau'n did flie:
Then praife the Shooter and the Shoote,
Which chang'd the world for better boote.

E 4   How

Epig.16 In Robertum Shute fil:Rob:Pre.

How faire yong *Shute* shootes at his fathers aime
A few such shootes,and *Shute* will win the game:
If *Shute* shoote on as now he doth begin,
With learnings arrow hee le cliue honours pin:
He le hit the whitewhich *Shute* shot at(his father)
He shootes beyond his vertues I thinke rather:
Thus shootes yong *Shute*, if then his father *Shute*
For him we chang'd,we need not ask much boot.

Epig.17 In Rubrionem & Rullum.

Rubrio, Rullus snout-faire *Septimel*,
Both lou'd alike, yet could not bring about, (rell
Their chiefe pretence,but needs they must appa-
Hir breech-torn husband.Now he walks throw-
The streetes,to tauernes goes,vnto a play, (out
Neuer at home saue on some feasting day:
   At noone,at night,by turnes enioy you still,
   Rubrio Rullus snout-faire *Septimell*.

If

Epig. 18 In Luciam.

If any maruaile why,
Luce selles her loue for gold:
Tis she may haue to buy
Her loue when she is old.

Epig. 19. In Georgium Meriton, & Georgium Mountaine.

Your entertaine (nor can I passe away)
Of *Essex* with farre-famed *Lelia*;
Nor fore the Queen your seruice on Queens day
When such a Maister with you beareth sway,
How can Queenes College euer then decay?
No. Yet Queenes College euermore hath beene
Is,and will be,of Colleges the Queene.

The

Epig.20. Ad Dudleum North.

The sparkling lust of a pretious stone,
Breedes often wonder to the looker on:
But the resplendance of this pearle is more,
If laid in gold enameld with ore:
Thy noble birth(yong *North*)doth shine as bright,
As doth a Christall in the darksome night:
   But learning in so faire and yong a molde,
   Is like a Christall stone in burnisht golde.

Epig.21 In Rudionem.

Yon goes a gallant which will get repute,
From head to heele in his Carnation sute,
Slops,dublet,stockings,shooes,hat,bād,& fether,
Red yard-long ribbin,see the youth coms hither,
Who left his Dutchman hose should be vnseene
Aboue his mid-thigh he his cloake doth pin:
   O that he had to his Carnation hose,
   (I wish him well)a faire rich crimson nose.

Honie

Epig 22. Ad Gulielmum Shakespear

Honie-tong'd *Shakespeare* when I saw thine issue
I swore *Apollo* got them and none other,
Their rosie-tainted features cloth'd in tissue,
Some heauen born goddesse said to be their mo-
Rose-checkt *Adonis* with his amber tresses,(ther:
Faire fire-hot *Venus* charming him to loue her,
Chaste *Lucretia* virgine-like her dresses, (her:
Prowd lust-stung *Tarquine* seeking still to proue
Romea Richard; more whose names I know not,
Their sugred tongues,and power attractiue beuty
Say they are Saints althogh that Sts they shew not
For thousands vowes to them subiectiue dutie:
They burn in loue thy childrē *Shakespear* het thē,
Go,wo thy Muse more Nymphish brood beget
(them.

Romeo

Epig. 23 *In Ed: Allen.*

Rome had her *Roscius* and her Theater,
Her *Terence*, *Plautus*, *Ennius* and *Meander*,
The first to *Allen*, *Phœbus* did transfer (land her,
The next, *Thames* Swans receiu'd fore he coulde
Of both more worthy we by *Phœbus* doome,
Then t' *Allen Roscius* yeeld, to *London Rome*.

Finis.

To the right worshipful, sir Thomas Gerrard knight, Marshall &c. ennobled with Learnings renowne, and Warres dignitie.

 Any meane Poets (Schollers chiefe patron) offered their wel-meaning Poems to Alexander, whose rudenesse hee pardoned. Some to Augustus, which he highly rewarded. Others to Cæsar which he kindly accepted: euen so (right Worshipful) as you striue to surpasse these in Chiualrie, I doe not doubt, but you will equall them in curtesie: and thus (boldly) I referre all to your Worships clemencie.

Ioh: Weeuer.

Epig. 1 *Ad Petrum Leigh de Vnderline Militem.*

THe ancient acts lou'd *Leigh*, yet vndergoes
Of his forefathers, Vnder whose old Line
Haue beene kept vnder *Englands* chiefest foes:
But if Death do not Vndergo the Line
Of life; which now so long and true spun, showy
Hee'le ouergo the Knights of Vnder-line:
And vnder few thus much I doe diuine,
His name will be call'd *Leigh* of Ouer-line.

Epig. 2 *In Rufum.*

Some say the soule within the braine close lies,
Some in the head, in th'hart some, som in the eies,
Others affirme it harbours in the breast,
Others wil haue it in the blood to rest:
  Gainst all Philosophers I do suppose,
  Rufus red soule lies hid in his red nose.
                                      Virginitie

Epig. 3 *In Stellam.*

Virginitie doth *Stella* still commend,
That for a virgine so she may be counted;
Virginitie she might though reprehend,
Since she with *Rufus* in the coach was mounted:
  For tell me *Stella* virgine as thou art,
  To beare a virgin, is t a virgins part?

Epig. 4 *In Iscum.*

Iscus, inuite your friends vnto good cheare,
When they before inuited are you heare:
But else inuite them not in one whole yeare.

                                      Charis

Epig.5 In Charin vestium ostentatorem.

Charis doth change his raiment thrice a day,
Belike because the weather is so hot,
Nay tis to shew his needle wrought array,
His golden breeches,and his cordwaine coate:
 I haue beene with him,neuer saw him sweate,
 But once at table when he was at meate.

Epig.6 Ad Quintum.

Thou askt one thing of me which I denied,
That one thing nothing was,then thou replied,
If it was nothing which thou askt of me,
Then nothing Quintus I denied to thee:
 Now yet for nothing,one thing Quintus know,
 For nothing something Quintus thou dost ow.

Is't

Epig.7 In Braggadochionem.

Did Braggadochio meete a man in field?
Tis true,he did,the way he could not shun:
And did he force great Brundon weapons yeeld;
Nay there he lies.To vntrusse when he begun,
He stole his weapons and away did run:
 Vaine is thy vaunt,and victorie vniust,
 Thou durst not stay till he his points vntrust,

Epig.8 In Rubrionem.

Rubrio followes learning,followes mony;
He followes pleasure, and doth folow glorie,
He followes goods,would follow God also,
He followes Thetis,Galetæa too:
 So let him follow follies iourney make,
 He may long follow e're he ouertake.

F

Is't

Epig.9 In Cumberlandiæ Comitem.

Ist true which saith the Pythagorean,
One soule doth animate another man?
Then doth Couragious Cumberland enioy
Vlysses soule th'eternall scourge of Troy:
For at his becke the windes commander bendeth
And on his full saile fortune still attendeth.
 Wherfore his name & his al-conquering hand,
 A fatall CVMBER to our enemies LAND.

Epig.10 Ad Nathanielem Fletcher.

If Iudgement,Wit,and Learning I would call,
My simple worke of Epigrams to view,
For Iudgement,Wit,and Learning, Fletcher shal
Be cal'd to reade my Epigrams anew:
But iudgement,wit,& learning shal not see them,
Left iudgement,wit,nor learning he find in them.

You

Epig.11 In Lippum.

You say he spendes all,nothing meanes to purse,
Yet for this fault most men excusde wil hold him
You spend iust nought;he ill doth,you do wurse;
And as your neighbours(Lippus)of late told him,
You spend your selfe vpon an errand whore,
He doth spend much,but Lippus,you spend more,

Epig.12 In Othonem.

I pray you(maisters)do but Otho note,
How for his lies he doth an Author quote,
Thus he begins; Tis true yea in good faith,
For as They say,and as the Fellow saith:
 But who e're heard of any that could tell,
 Where Othoe's (they)or(fellow)yet did dwell.

F 2

Who

Epig. 13 In Galbum.

Who fees not *Galbus* both to bow and crouch
Vnto my Lo.( )horfes and his coach: (forth,
And faies (God bleffe them) when they do come
And thou(fair coach)proud of my L.great worth,
    He giues him noght:here *Galbus* heare we fhal
Curfe his great horfes,coach,my Lo.and all.

Epig. 14 In Pontum.

This golden Foole,and filken Affe you fee,
In euery point a woman faine would be:
He weares a fanne,and fhewes his naked breft,
And with a partlet his Cranes necke is dreft:
Giue him a maske,for certes hee's afeard,
Left fun,or wind,fhould weather-beat his beard:
    Thus when he weares a partlet,maske,and fan,
Is *Pontus* then a woman,or a man?

Great

Epig. 15 In Nauium.

Great *Nauius* still bids many vnto meate,
His meate is raw that no man can it eate:
All in a chafe,findes fault and ftrikes the Cooke,
That to his meate he did no better looke.
    Yet this poore Cooke is in no fault I know,
For certes *Nauius* bade him roft it raw.

Epig. 16 Ad Thomam Holecroft De Vaile Reiall Armis.

Doth *Valorous Holecroft* royalize *Vaile Roiall*,
Or doth *Vaile Royall* royalize his name?
His deedes too great vnuail'd to fhew his triall,
Then through a Vaile Ile royalize his fame:
    Thus from Vaile Royal borrow I the vaile,
To hide his vertues when my wit doth faile.

F 3   Thou

Epig. 17 In Iellam.

Thou haft a vice if I may call it one,
Nor good,nor honeft,yet a vice alone,
To come from *London* thou wilt neuer miffe,
Only thy friends to fauour with a kiffe:
    But *Iella* thou doft only that man fauor, (uor.
    Thou doft not kiffe nor trouble with thy fla-

Epig. 18 De Rollo.

Perforce(*Rollo* faid)from *Sull* a kiffe he tooke,
And twixt her lips his foul (not knowing)left him
But then he fent his heart his foule to looke,
And her bright ey-beams of his heart bereft him:
If with that kiffe he had not drawn a breath,
Whereby fuftaind his fouleleffe body is,
Th it day had beene his difmall day of death,
Wherein he fnatcht from chafed *Sull* a kiffe:
    Tis ftrange her kiffe was then fo pleafing cold,
    When with the beft fhe burnt the boy of old.
Whofe

Epig. 19 In Vulpem puritanum.

Whofe lauifh-tongu'd precifme will not fpare,
The chiefeft pillars of our cleargie men,
But to a caft of counters them compare,
Giuing no count with Counters nor with pen:
Nor can I count the waies he doth abufe them,
Though late he had beene in the Counter caft,
If that his cheefe caft had not bin to vfe them,
And craue their friendfhip,for his words or'epaft:
And if caft counters yet he be not giuing,
His caft of counters cafts away his liuing.

Epig. 20 De Mella.

From one eie alwaies *Mella* teares do fall,
And what's the caufe? She hath but one in all.

F 4   Thou

Epig. 21 *In Sippum.*

Thou cal'st thy selfe Knight, *Sippus* of the Poste,
But on the pillor-I say knighthoods lost,
Yet as thou dost for six pence cut a throate,
At *Westminster* be periur'd for a groate:
Cheate and Cros-bite, to all men do but euill,
Thou maist be knight, and ride poste to the deuil.

Epig. 22 *Ad Gulielmum Grantam.*

Suffize it *Grantam* that I *Grantam* name
And say yong *Grantam* wil keep *Grantams* fame:
Thy very name Antiquitie sets forth,
And *Grantam* proues a man of noble worth:
    Thus do I glaunce at *Grantam*; *Grantam* then
    Doth grant too great a subiect for my pen.

He

Epig. 23 *Ad Iohannem Egerton.*

He that would garnish with a seuerall light
Thy seuerall vertues, and in praise them dight:
He should not want that wittie treasures store,
Which Muses gaue to *Homer* once of yore:
But wit I want, therefore Ile spare my song,
Left poore in praise, thou count me rich in wrong

Epig. 24 *Ad Henricum Porter.*

Porter, I durst not mell with sacred Writ,
Nor woe the Mistris fore I win the maide,
For my yong yeeres are taskt, its yet vnsitte
For youth, as eld is neuer halfe so staid,
Thy selfe which hath the summe of Art and Wit
Thus much I know vnto me would haue said:
    Thy siluer bell could not so sweetly sing,
    If that too soone thou hadst begun her ring.

Thou

To the right worshipful, sir Cut-
bert Halsey knight, perfected with
the ornament of Honor, and
titles of Nobilitie.

 Good wit (right *Worshipful*) wil shew
his vigour in any subiect, and trauell
as easily ouer a mountaine as a mole-
hill. But mine (vnworthy the title of
wit) tyred within three steppes of the
mountaines foote, lay plodding there this long, and now
at the last, hath brought forth a mouse: if you chance
to ride this way, you cannot chuse but laugh, and the
pleasant remembrance of this strange sight wil beguile
the times hast, and shorten the wayes length: and (perhaps) when you come home, serue for a boorde-ieast:
which if it do, I shalbe satisfied.

        Ioh: Weeuer.

Epig. 1 *Ad Richardum Houghton Militem.*

IF that my pen were of the wing of Fame,
And Gods immortall Nectar for my inke;
Then could I canonize great *Houghtons* name:
Til the my Muse speaks not what she doth think
Long shuld'st thou liue in thy gold-gilded tower
If that my Muse could keep thee stil from death:
Long bathe thy selfe in that thy blissefull bower,
If my waste paper could but lend thee breath:
Yet this my duty doe not hold in scorne;
My Muse hereafter may thy praise adorne.

Epig. 2 *Ad Lectorem.*

Reader, this sift last weeke in dead mens praise
I would not spend one line, becaufe i spied,
That more then halfe the week were fasting dais,
And that thou wert already mortified:
Remember yet (kind Reader) if thou can,
Thou art no more than any mortall man.

Sicke-

The sixt weeke.

Epig. 3 In tumulum Thomæ Houghton Armig.

Sicke sad-fac'd Sorrow mixt with maladie,
Vpon this tombe now pitch thy cole-black tent,
Heart-breaking groanes and howling miserie,
Be as Cares canons from Griefes castle sent,
Gainst Deaths pauilion all make batterie.
In *Houghtons* death. Death lōg before death went
Vnrest, pain, anguish, sighs, sobs, tears be coūting
Vntill some write *Dianæs* three dayes hunting

Epig. 4 In Gulielmum Houghton.

Faine would faire *Venus* sport her in thy face,
But *Mars* forbids her his sterne marching place:
Then comes that heauēnly harbinger of *Ioue*,
And ioyns with *Mars* & with the queen of *Loue*
And thus three gods these gifts haue giuen thee,
Valour, wit, fauour, and ciuilitie.

Galla

The fifth weeke.

Epig. 5 In Gallam.

Galla with mutton and pottage vsde to pray,
A month together saue one *Venus* day:
But now her purenes *Lenton* meate doth fast,
Three *Venus* daies in one weeke found at last:
  And yet she saith there are too few by three,
  Galla would haue all *Venus* daies to be.

Epig 6 In Sullum.

Thou hast desir'd me *Sullus* oft indeede,
To thy friend *Mat* to do thy commendations,
I would do more if that thou stoode in neede,
Amongst acquaintance these are only fashions:
  Yet wish me not commend thee to thy friend,
  For I know nought in thee I can commend.

My

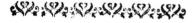

The sixt weeke.

Epig. 7

My *Cosens* life (I heare) is new out dated,
And all his pounds could not pay for two yeares,
And two rich *Plutoe's*, for his goods which waited
Snatcht them from me (*a crosse that all men bears*)
  But ti's no matter, for goods gotten euil,
  Pluto wil haue, or else some other deuill.

Epig. 8 In tumulum Iuelli.

Here lyeth *Iuell*, who knoweth not the rest,
Is worthie to be ignorant at least.

Be

The sixt weeke.

Epig. 9 In tumulum Ferdinand. Darbie.

Be not so bould to ope this dead mans dore,
Vnlesse thou come from th'aërie house of woes,
Ne dare thou once vpon this Marble pore,
Vnlesse thou poure thy sight out on these roes,
If to faire knighthood thou bearst any zeale,
Vnrest, care, griefe, sad discontent, and woe,
On these fiue bells ring thou a dolefull peale,
Volies of sighes fast after them let goe:
Rest, in vnrest, teares-spitting forge be burning,
Vntill some write *The Muses nine dayes mourning*.

Epig. 10 Ad Samuelem Daniel.

Daniel, thou in tragicke note excells,
As *Rosamond* and *Cleopatra* tells:
Why dost thou not in a drawne bloudy line,
Offer vp teares at *Ferdinandoes* shrine?
  But those that e're he di'de bewitcht him then,
  Belike bewitcheth now each Poets pen.

Marston

Epig.11 Ad Io: Marston, & Ben: Iohnson.

Marston, thy Muse enharbours *Horace* vaine,
Then some *Augustus* giue thee *Horace* merit,
And thine embuskin'd *Iohnson* doth retaine
So rich a stile, and wondrous gallant spirit;
That if to praise your Muses I desired,   (mired
My Muse would muse. Such wittes must be ad-

Epig.12 In tumulum Auari.

Here lieth he who neuer aught
  To man or woman gaue:
And now it grieues him that thou read'st
  For nought this on his graue.

Liue

Epig.13 Ad Gulielmum Warner.

Liue prince of Poets, thy affections guide,
Where Witte attires her selfe in Vertues sute,
Whilst *Enolads* fame thy flowing verse doth pride
This be thy praise: Thy *Albions* absolute.

Epig.14 In tumulum Abrahami Simple.

Within this place lies *Abraham* the *Ciuil*,
Who neuer did good, who neuer did euill:
Too ill then for God, too good for the deuill.

Epig.15 in Asinum quendam.

You know (sir Asse) how you did me annoy,
To steale away my little tale of *Troy*:
And asking for it, you all in a fume,
Twixt two bigge jawes did wholy it consume:
  To be destroy'd *Troyes* fortune sure it was,
  Once with an Horse, againe now with an Asse.

G   Foule

Epig.16 In Rufum

Foule red nosde *Rufus*, fauour thou maist gaine,
If with his children thou would take some paine:
But vntill *Rufus* fauour fairer be,
He should not giue his fauour vnto me.

Epig.17 In Zoilum.

Zoilus, thou laugh'st but onely when I weepe,
And when I laugh that's weeping cheer for thee,
Then weeping *Zoilus* I will thee keepe,
My booke and me still laughing thou shalt see:
  Now quickly *Zoilus* take vp thy four quarters,
  And like a knaue goe hang thee in thy garters.

The

Epig.18 In obitum Thoma Fisher à Io: Fishrocci.

The Fisher did the fish so dearely loue,
That stil he gaue the fish fresh wormes to eate,
O then what should the fish so nearely moue,
To giue the fisher to the wormes for meate?

Epig.19 In Scyllam

By Lord nor Ladie *Scylla* will not sweare,
By God nor goddesse, nor so great a thing,
Yet she commits a greater fault I feare,
In swearing alwaies by her faire gold ring.

G 2   Nor

Epig.20 In Cynam.

Nor you did ſweare not once ſince you were born
Yet at each word you ſay you will be ſworne:
A fault you get whilſt you a fault would flie,
For when you ſweare not, *Cyna* then you lie.

Epig. 21 Liber ad Authorem.

I'm likt of many, many me approue,
Some like me not, for thy ſake ne me loue:
I do not care: who makes a banquet lookes
To pleaſe his gueſts, & not to pleaſe the Cookes.

But

Epig.22. In Gulielmum Rich: Cantabr: procu.

But that I am too poore to pen thy praiſe,
I would preſume thy glorious name to raiſe:
Beyond the riches of the Indian land,
Worth more then worthleſſe *Tagus* golden ſand:
But O thy vertues paſſe my praiſes pitch,
Thy learnings fame aboue thy name is rich:
How wel then Vertue ſorts her with thy fame
That art both rich in Art, and *Rich* in Name.

Epig.23 In obitum Ed. Spencer Poetæ preſtantiſſ.

Colin's gone home, the glorie of his clime,
The Muſes Mirrour, and the Shepheards Saint;
Spencer is ruin'd, of our latter time
The faireſt ruine, Faëries fouleſt want:
Then his *Time-ruines* did our ruine ſhow,
Which by his ruine we vntimely know:
Spencer therfore thy *Ruines* were cal'd in,
Too ſoone to ſorrow leaſt we ſhould begin.

G 3   *Thornton.*

Epig.24 Ad Iacobum Thornton.

Thornton well read, ſay not I do thee wrong,
In that I haue deſer'd thy praiſe ſo long,
Thy gentleman-like parts when as I find,
With thy graue ſtudies, all in one combinde:
 Faine would I praiſe thee, but I ſee my skill,
 Is now defectiue to my great good will.

Epig. 25 In Ed: Wrightington.

If vertuous youth now in his chiefeſt prime,
To vertues loue be wholy thus addicted,
What doth graue eld, with milke-white haires in time?
Aſſure vs of one vice to be afflicted?
 For by and by the plant doth ſtraight appeare,
 Which afterward great ſtore of fruit will beare.

Ames prodigall reporte (right Wor.) of your admired curteſie, and the no leſſe vertuous then valorous diſpoſition of Leighs antique family, (in whoſe praiſe a better Poet might (ſpend whole quiers of paper) perſwade me you will reade ouer theſe few Epigrammes, though farre differing from other wittes, preſented to the view of your Worſhip. And weigh withal well affected good will : ſo ſhall I attaine my long deſired wiſh, and the end of this my worke.

1

Ioh: Weeuer.

G 4   Gerard

Epig.1 Ad Thomam Gerard Militem.

GErard,among the labours of my quill,
  Which my glad Muse presumingly hath writ,
As one right worthie thee commend I will,
For valour,wisedome, bountihood and wit:
But valiant Gerard, thee or thine to praise,
Is for to praise the star-bespangled skie,
Fame long agoe vnto the heau ns did raise!
Thy rare exploits and Mars-like Chiualrie:
  Sith by thy deedes thy praise abroad doth flie,
  Thy selfe commends thy selfe,then need not I.

Epig 2 In carum fictum amicum.

Dost thou thinke Chloes hee's a faithfull friend,
For whô this wondrous cheer thou dost prouide?
No:he but loues so long as thou wilt spend
Thy beefe and brawne,if that the truth were tride
  If euery day I should so costly dine,
  Carus I know would be a friend of mine.

Sparsus

Epig.3 In Sparsum.

Sparsus thou'rt sicke ten times a yeere and more,
Yet not thy selfe,but vs, thy sicknesse hu ts,
When thou recouers wee looke euermore,
For thy releefe some Pretour to disburse:
  Fie,in one yeere be sicke but once vnneath,
  And when thou'rt sicke Sparsus be sicke to death.

Epig.4 In Pontum

This for a wonder many men haue made,
That Pontus house so many chimnies had:
The workmans skil I for the wonder tooke,
Which made thê so that few could see thê smoak.

Did

Epig. 5 In Hugonem.

Did not once thine old familiar friend
Chypus, desire thee ten pounds to him lend;
Sir I haue none (saidst thou) so God me saue,
Yet for his horse eu'n then ten pound thou gauet
Thus for ten pounds thou'lt sooner trust a horse,
Than thy dear friend; &:be forsworn,thats worse.

Epig.6 In eundem

And dost thou thinke thou offers Claius right,
In causing him ten pounds of debt to pay,
Because that Boscus ran the other night
With twenty-hundred in thy debt away:
  If thou canst lose by Boscus twentie : then
  In faith by Claius thou may well lose ten.

L.

Lacus

Epig. 7. In Lacum

Lacus I saw a cruell Cappe still weare,
(O cruell cap that pulles away his haire)
I wondred much what plague had so him crost,
That both on chin and head all was quite lost:
A new disease (some said) a dry hot cold;
Yet this disease a thousand yeere was old.

Epig.8. In Portianum

Portian is taken for a traueller:
Why? For he weares a gold ring in his eare,
Certes and if a ring may be a signe,
Who better traueller than his mothers swine?
They in their Nose, he in his Ears;
Whether then is the better traueller?
Grillus I wot hath deeper gone then he,
If he hath further gone, they euen be.

But

Epig. 9

But wodden chalices of yore,
Yet golden priests were then great store,
Now golden chalices we make,
For wodden priests in hand to take:
Lets cast our priests in a new molde,
Or else for wood lets change our golde.

Epig. 10 *In Cacum*

Cacus is angry he hath not a place
Amongst the Worthies of our Faërie land,
Nor doth the pesant thinke himselfe too base,
Among the brauest of the Lordes to stand:
Hee weares braue clothes; but what weares hee
An Asse an Asse is in a Lions skin. (within?

Des-

Epig. 11 *Ad Musam suam, de obitu fortis-* *simi insignisq, iuuenis Thomæ Eger-* *ton militis.*

Descend my Muse into the bed of Death,
(Embalming first his body with thy teares)
And chide the Fates vntill they lend him breath,
Because they rapt him in his youthfull yeares;
Yet stay my Muse, Fates offred him no wrong,
In vertue old he was, in yeeres though yong.

Epig. 12 *In Quintum.*

To giue a booke thou saist I may do well, (sell.
Yet thou n'ere readst a book, before a book thou

Ex-

Epig. 13 *In Tubrionem*

Extramnemers or Watermen giue roome,
For by his feather *Tubrioe's* spied to come.
A Sculler sir; here is a paire of Oares:
Ist please your Worship, I did speake before:
I'm your first man; he lies, here is my boate:
Your Worship lands at Pauls wharfe, doth it not
No, Westminster; O foole, dost thou not know,
That gainst the wind thou cannot *Tubrio* row?

Epig. 14 *Ad Cordredum.*

O impudent! a liuing! for whose sake?
This meanes to my Lord( )dost thou make?
Fie; thus; to beg thy selfe, *One of rare parts
I am* (my Lord) *beside Maister of Arts,* .

And:

And: Go no further; thou art too short leg'd,
And beg no more, lest thou thy selfe be beg'd:
Yet (*Cordred*) thou shalt haue (do not despaire)
The Vicarage of Saint Fooles at Steeple faire.

Epig. 15 *Satyricum in Audrian lanam.*

Looke to your selfe, I'le whip you mistris *Audrie*,
For keeping such a brothel house of ( )
Is't true indeede? hath *Sulla* learn'd thy skill?
Dri'de veines and arteries with pure blood to fil;
In drinking cordialls fearing to be too old,
Of Amber-greece prepared pearle and gold:
Mandrake, Eringe and Potatie rootes,
Fiue pound a weeke in Poticaries bookes:
Oh stay, no more; for *Audria* I heare tell
Is new become a bride, but in *Bridewell.*

O chide

The ſeuenth weeke

Epig. 16 Ad Richardum Houghton Militem

O chide me not, for that I doe enroule
Thy worthy name here (Houghton) in the end,
For now I hope none will my booke controule,
Leſt thine heroicke ſpirit they offend,
Cloſe with thy Vertues then this ſeely ſcroule,
That praiſe on thee, and it, may euer tend:
   Which if it doe I will aduenture then,
   To take a taske fit for a golden pen.

Epig. 17 Ad Lectorem.

If in the firſt thou count me worthy blame,
Yet pardon me, thus Homer did offend,
If in the midſt, then Pedo I can name,
Cherill in all, Getulicus in th'end.
   Thy fauour (Reader) then obtaine I ſhall,
   I am but bad i'th firſt, midſt, end, and all.

Finis.

G8b

Notes on the *Epigrammes*

The purpose of these notes is to give biographical information. Full references are cited for unpublished archive material, but not for facts taken from my chief printed sources (Venn's *Alumni Cantabrigienses*, the *Dictionary of National Biography*, Hasler's *The House of Commons 1558–1603*, and McKerrow's edition of *Epigrammes* (M.)). Where no source is indicated, I usually follow Venn; and the first date for Cambridge students refers to matriculation or to admission to a college, as in Venn. In the case of joke epigrams I suggest possible identifications with a question mark in brackets (?): I do not claim that I have unriddled all of Weever's names correctly, but only that these are some of the names that would spring to mind in Cambridge in the 1590s.

For abbreviations see pp. ix–x.

Title-page *first seuen*] Weever evidently hoped to publish another collection.
Sit voluisse, Sat valuisse] Also found on the title-page of *Faunus*. 'Not traced; not classical; possibly invented by Weever ... meaning something like "May my having desired [to please] be sufficient merit"' (Davenport, ed. *Faunus*).

V. S. for Thomas Bushell] For Simmes and Bushell see p. 23 ff.
A2 *Dedication*] For Hoghton see *Lost Years*, Ch. II. Hoghton was knighted in late June 1599, and ceased to be sheriff in late November 1599: the dedication was written between these dates.
11. *seated ... curtesie*] From the *Arcadia*

(ed. 1621, p. 8; Crawford, *apud* M.). Weever borrowed extensively from *Arcadia* in *Faunus*.

A3b *T. B. Gen.*] Perhaps T. Bastard (M.); or T. Bell, a pensioner at Queens' (1595)?

A4a *Grant*] Granta. Cambridge was formerly 'Grantabridge'.

Tho: Kedgewin] Pensioner at Emmanuel, 1594.

A4b *Ed: Gurney*] Pensioner at Queens', 1594 (Venn; *DNB*); later well known as a divine. Probably from a higher social level than Weever; dedicating *Corpus Christi* (1619) to his godfather, Gurney mentioned 'your two daughters, my cousin Yelverton, and the Lady Strange'.

A4b *In ... Authoris*] It is 'impossible to emend these lines satisfactorily, as there is no means of knowing what standard of correctness we should expect from their author' (M., with some suggested corrections).

A5a *M. Milward*] 'Possibly Matthias Milward, a scholar of St John's. See *DNB*' (M.). BA, 1594–5; MA, 1598.

15. *twenty ... months*] Cf. p. 87.

A5b 8. *Twixt ... tong*] Cf. *The Rape of Lucrece*, 679: 'Entombs her outcry in her lips' sweet fold.'

17. *Nor ... dayes*] Written, presumably, before Weever settled in London.

A6a *Delians*] Apollo's (Delian, because born in Delos); or Samuel Daniel's (author of *Delia*, 1592).

stanza 3. *Must I ... beaten*] Apparently added in 1599. Alludes to the epistle before Hall's *Virgidemiae* headed 'His defiance to Envy', and to the epistle before Marston's *Scourge of Villainy*, headed 'To Detraction I present my Poesy' (M.). T. M.'s *Micro-cynicon* (1599) also begins with 'His defiance to Envy'.

15. *Castilioe's*] A name much used in Marston's *Poems* (see pp. 220–21).

A6b 13. *Tubro*] 'Tubrio' is found in Marston (*Poems*, pp. 223–6); cf. vii. 13.

A7a 5–6. *being ... printed*] See p. 88.

9. *yeere of Iubile*] Cf. *Faunus*, l. 1680: 'It was the secular Jubilee of the Roman Church, celebrated from 1300; and always the occasion of special pilgrimages to Rome.' See *OED*, Jubilee, 1: (Jewish History) ... A year of emancipation and restoration ... to be

kept every fifty years. The phrase recurs in Weever's 'prophecy' for 1600 (*Faunus*, p. 68), and this suggests that the *Epigrammes* were finally printed late in 1599, and here refer to 1600.

11. *I keep no order*] Cf. *Funeral Monuments* (p. 73, above).

A8 This leaf is missing in O and H; see p. 86.

i.1. *choplog*] one who chops logic.

broch] tusk, tooth (*OED*, 8; first recorded 1607).

Parnassus] i.e. Cambridge.

Massicke] wine of Mount Massicus, in Campania. Cf. Martial, iii.49.

i.5. *Crassus*] (?) William Crashaw, Fellow of St John's from 1594.

i.6. *Brillus*] (?) Titus Bright, pensioner at Emmanuel, 1597.

Bases] *OED*: base, 2: a plaited skirt, of cloth, velvet, or rich brocade, appended to the doublet, and reaching from the waist to the knee, common in the Tudor period.

i.7. *Sheeps greene*] 'At Cambridge, on the south-west of the town, between Newnham Mill and the Granta' (M.). Bridge street: also in Cambridge.

warrant] the official licence required for printing new books.

printeth ... hose] *OED*: print, 12: to stamp or mark a textile fabric with a pattern.

i.8 *Thyrus*] *Tyros Roring Megge* ('planted against the walls of melancholy'), 1598, by Tom Tyro, apparently a Cambridge man, was printed by V. Simmes, and included epigrams. Perhaps Weever referred to a known contemporary. (Venn has a 'Thomas Tyroe', BA 1619, born in 1598.)

i.11. *Boscus*] Cf. vii.6, and *OED*: bosk, bosky: a bush; small wood. There were many men called Wood at Cambridge; also Samuel Bush (sizar at Trinity, 1596).

i.12. *hare*] So also Martial (xiii.92).

i.13. *Roger Manners*] 'Fifth earl of Rutland, 1576–1612. Succeeded to the earldom in 1588. Educated for a time at Queens' ... but in 1590 removed to Corpus Christi' (M.). See also p. 9, *DNB*.

i.15. *Monoceros*] (?) Thomas Horne, sizar at Queens' (1596).

i.16. *Poenus*] (?) W. Penny, sizar at Trinity (1596). *Clari-cords*] A perverted

form of clavichord; also 'clarigol'; i.e.
whips, which could be 'stringed
instruments' (M.; *Parnassus Plays*, p. 195,
note). Constables] (?) John Constable,
pensioner at Queens', 1596.

i.17. *Felix*] (?) N. Gladman; sizar at
Trinity, *c*. 1598.

i.19] Cf. p. 37; and *Parnassus Plays*, p.
314—a wife 'can wear a hood like a
hawk'.

i.21. *Florella*] 'From 1592 to 1595
Florimond Peraux ... of Orleans, a
licentiate of civil law, lived and gave
lectures in Hebrew' at Queens' (Searle, p.
389). Perhaps 'Florella' was connected
with him.

i.23. *Drayton*] Cf. p. 22. Drayton
greatly admired Sidney (*Drayton*, p. 87,
ftn.).

B7 *Robert Dalton of Pilling*] This must
be Robert Dalton of Thurnham Hall,
Esq., who died in 1615, and whose
mother was Anne, daughter of Sir
Richard Molyneux of Sefton (cf. p. 9).
He seems to have been 'of Pilling' and 'of
Thurnham' (see *Dalton v. Hoghton*, 44
Elizabeth, DL4.44.5). *Richard* Dalton of
Pilling (cf. p. 33), a Fellow Commoner at
Queens' (1595), who was tutored, like
Weever, by W. Covell, was probably
Robert's son.

ii.2. *Torto*] (?) H. Torte, formerly a
sizar at Queens' (1567), became vicar of
Bassingbourne, near Cambridge, in 1598.
Or a quibble on 'torqueo' (twist, bend):
(?) Francis Bendish (Jesus, 1594) or (?)
William Bendish (Jesus, 1594).

ii.5. *Great Marcus*] (?) Anthony
Markham, Fellow Commoner at Caius
(1594), or George Markeham, Fellow
Commoner at Caius (1593), or John
Marcham, pensioner at St John's (1595).

ii.6. *Ruffinus*] 'Cf. *The Spanish
Tragedy*, IV.iv.216 ... but of course
Hieronymo is not made to speak
afterwards' (M.). Ruffin was a surname
at this time; F. Ruffin matriculated at
Oxford in 1604.

ii.8. *Cario*] Could be connected with A.
Carr (St John's, 1594), R. Carr (Trinity,
1596), T. Carr (St John's, 1595), or W.
Carr (St John's, 1595).

ii.10. *Nihil ... desunt*] Vergil, *Eclogues*,
viii.67 (M.).

ii.9. *old-cook*] cuckold. Miles *Raven*
was a Fellow of King's (1590–1612); 'fair

Fulva' (?Fulvia) could have been a
mistress rather than a wife.

ii.11. *D. D. Palmer*] Either John Palmer
(BA, 1571–2; MA, 1575; DD, 1595;
Master of Magdalene, 1595–1604) or
William Palmer (BA, 1559–60, MA, 1563;
DD, 1598). See Venn, *DNB*, M.

ii.12. *Castilio*] See A6a, note.

ii.14] See p. 15.

ii.15. *Stratus*] A pun on 'sterno'
('stratus'), spread out, stew, throw down,
lay low? Perhaps R. Strode (St John's
1597–8), or John Downe, Fellow of
Emmanuel (from 1594).

ii.16] See iv.3. Humphrey Tyndall,
President of Queens' (1579–1614), was
presented to the vicarage of Soham,
Cambridgeshire, in 1577. His sister
married Edward Upcher of Soham
(Searle, p. 363 ff.), and Richard Upcher
probably belonged to the same family.

ii.17. *Calvus*] (?) D. Wigmore, sizar at
Queens' (May 1592); BA, 1595–6; or T.
Baldwin (St John's, 1594).

white beare] Paris Garden was known
for its bear-baiting, but here a prostitute
is meant. 'Knave's Acre was in Soho,
apparently part of Brewer Street. For
Cuckold's Haven, on the Thames below
Greenwich, cf. Nares, *Glossary*' (M.).

ii.18. *Mirmedon*] OED, myrmidon, 2: a
faithful follower. 3: a hired ruffian (first
in 1649). 'Men of France': cf. ii.21.

ii.19. *lurcher*] OED, 1: a glutton; 2: a
petty thief, swindler or rogue.

ii.21. *Gullio*] (?) John Gouldson,
pensioner at Queens', 1594. His tutor
was Clement *French*, Fellow of Queens'
(1592–1601). For the allusion to this
epigram in *The Return from Parnassus*
see p. 51. Davenport thought that
'Gullio' and Hall's 'Gullion' are 'clearly
meant for the same man' (Hall, *Poems*,
pp. 189–90). With '159 and 8' cf. *Tyros
Roring Megge*, 1598, B3a; *The Wipping
of the Satyre*, p. 19; and other books of
this period.

ii.22] Perhaps 'Coa will never see God
till she has been revived at Pie Corner'?
('Every eye shall see him ... I am Alpha
and Omega ... saith the Lord',
Revelation, i.7–8).

ii.24] 'In certain methods of voting by
ballot among the Greeks the letter T is
said to have stood for acquittal, Θ for
condemnation, and Λ for deferring of

judgement' (M.).

C8 *Sir Richard Molyneux*] Of Sefton, Lancs.; brother-in-law of Sir Richard Hoghton, Sir Peter Leigh, Sir Thomas Gerard; cousin of Robert Dalton and Sir Edward Warren; close friend and business associate of Sir Cuthbert Halsall. Born *c.* 1559; knighted 1586; baronet 1611; died 1623. High Sheriff of Lancs., 1588–9, 1596–7. (See Hasler.)

iii.1. *Moone*] Probably William Moone, Fellow of St Catharine's, and Senior Proctor, 1597–8. See p. 14.

iii.3. *Mounteagle*] William Parker (1575–1622), known by courtesy as Lord Monteagle in right of his mother (*DNB*); knighted by Essex in Ireland (July 1599), hence 'now thy country's pride'. Gave warning of the Gunpowder Plot in 1605, after receiving an anonymous letter. For his family connection with Sir Thomas Langton see p. 9.

iii.4. *Bunas*] As this is a man, perhaps a misprint for Greek 'bounos', a hill or mound; (?) George Mountain, Fellow of Queens' (cf. iv.19) or Richard Hill, pensioner at Queens', 1596.

iii.5. *In Ramistas*] A 'nonsensical statement about the Ramists' (M.); so perhaps it is not about the Ramists, but about R. Lambkin (pensioner at Queens', 1593), or T. Ram (Fellow of King's, 1591–1601). For the exceptional rains from 1594 to 1598 see above, p. 14. Searle noted that there was 'a great flood' at Cambridge in 1594, and that the beer at Queens' was lost; other floods followed in 1596–7 (pp. 386–7). 'Single' beer was inferior in quality (*OED*, 'single', 13). 'Sturbridge, a place just north of Cambridge, was the site of a fair held annually for a fortnight from 19 September ... it was one of the greatest fairs in England (Marston, *Poems*, p. 302).

iii.7] These allusions to Greek mythology, etc., are parodies, or mere verbal fooling. I am reminded of Marston's inflated style, and of Furor Poeticus in the *Parnassus Plays*.

iii.9. *Battus*] (?) H. Bate (Emmanuel, 1593), or N. Bate (St John's, 1596), or R. Bate (BA from Trinity, 1597–8).

iii.10. *De Ore*] (?) J. Oraford (pensioner, Queens', 1597).

iii.13. *Rodering*] (?) John Rodeknight,

Fellow of Queens', 1592–1605. 'He was one of those who "went overseas" in 1594' (Venn), hence perhaps 'road erring'. *Beard*: perhaps Thomas Beard (BA, Jesus, 1587–8; BD, 1602), author of *The theatre of God's judgements* (1597).

iii.20] Cf. p. 15.

iii.21] A George Grave matriculated at Trinity, 1577–8; BA, 1582–3. Ordained deacon and priest, 1579; canon of Algarkirk, Lincs., 1579; rector of Sotby, Lincs., 1585 (Venn).

iii.22. *Covel*] For William Covell, Weever's first tutor at Queens', see pp. 17; BA, 1584: MA, 1588; DD, 1601; he became a Fellow in 1589. See also *DNB*. Compare *Faunus*, p. 17: 'words to beryl straight distilled'.

iii.23. *D. D. Ouerall*] 'John Overall, 1560–1619. He became regius professor of Divinity at Cambridge and DD in 1596. From 1598 to 1607 master of St Catharine's Hall' (M.). He succeeded William Whitaker, regius professor of Divinity, 1580–95. See *DNB* for both. Whitaker was a Calvinist and puritan, Overall a moderate in church affairs.

D7b *sir Edward Warren*] Of Poynton, Cheshire, and Woodplumpton, Lancs.; 1563–1609. Sheriff of Cheshire, 1597–8; JP, Lancs., 1598. At Woodplumpton, Warren was a near neighbour of Henry Butler, Weever's uncle (cf. H. Fishwick, *The History of the Parish of St Michaels-on-Wyre* (CS, 1891, XXV, 202 ff.)). In Hasler.

iv.1] For Henry Butler see above, p. 4, and *Lost Years*, pp. 51, 147.

iv.2] (?) George Deacon, pensioner at Queens', 1595.

iv.3] On 26 March 1599, Captain John Upcher, captain of 200 soldiers in the Low Countries, acknowledged that he was contracted to Elizabeth Lynne and intended very shortly to marry her; by 19 August 1599, he was dead (PCC; 67 Kidd). A John Upcher was pensioner at Queens' from 1582. See also ii.16.

iv.4. *Ro: Allot*] Sizar, St John's, *c.* 1592; BA, 1595–6; MA and Fellow, 1599. Linacre lecturer. A celebrated physician (Venn; *DNB*). Cf. p. 22.

Chr. Middleton] Sizar, St John's, 1587; Ba, *c.* 1600 (Venn; *DNB*). Cf. p. 22.

iv. 5] Thomas Oxborough, pensioner at Queens', 1594.

cancelleere] 'One or two turns upon the wing made by a hawk, in order to recover herself before striking. This is the earliest example [in *OED*]' (M.).

iv.6] 'Sutor': shoemaker; 'faber': workman, smith, carpenter. Probably refers to a known individual.

iv.8] 'Palmo' could be someone called Palmer, or ('palmes', a vine-sprout) J. Viney, sizar at St John's, *c.* 1594.

iv.9] Cf. Martial, xiii.2: 'you may be as keen-nosed as you please; in a word, you may be all nose'; also Catullus, xiii. 13–14.

iv.10 *Steron*] If a student, perhaps John Stearne is meant (pensioner at St John's, *c.* 1595). 'Legislator' could be ironic.

iv.11] (?) John or Philip Spurling (pensioners at Trinity, *c.* 1596).

iv.12] For Hugo, cf. vii.5.

iv.13] 'Thomas Playfere, 1561?–1609. Lady Margaret professor of Divinity at Cambridge in 1596 ... It is not clear whether he was commonly called "Mellifluous Plaifer" or whether Weever is alluding to a passage in Nashe's *Strange News*, 1592, sig. I3v, where this name is given to him' (M.; *DNB*).

iv.14 *Matho*] (?) Tobie Matthew (1546–1628), Bishop of Durham, 1595, and Archbishop of York, 1606, had already held many church-livings in 1599: archdeacon of Bath, 1572; dean of Christ Church, 1576; precentor of Salisbury, 1583; installed dean of Durham, 1583; resigned deanery of Christ Church, 1584 (*DNB*).

Gnidus] Perhaps from 'cnide', 'gnide', a nettle: (?) connected with Stephen Nettles, Pensioner at Queens', 1595.

iv.15] Robert Shute: probably at Peterhouse, *c.* 1542; Gray's Inn, 1550; Reader, 1568; Treasurer, 1576; Recorder of Cambridge 1558–90; Baron of the Exchequer, 1579–86; Queen's Bench, 1586–90; Second Justice and Chief Justice at Lancaster (R. Somerville, *History of the Duchy of Lancaster*, 1953, pp. 471, 474); died 1590.

iv.16] Fourth son of the preceding. Matriculated at Christ's, 1598–9 (M.). Another Robert Shute was Fellow Commoner at Queens' from 1588 (Venn).

iv.19. *Meriton*] Fellow of Queens' (1589–1600); junior bursar, 1595–6, and senior bursar, 1596–7; BD, 1596; DD,

1601. Later Dean of Peterborough and Dean of York. Died 1624. See *DNB*.

Mountaine] Fellow of Queens' (1592–1611); BA 1589–90; MA, 1593; DD, 1607. Chaplain to Earl of Essex, and attended him on the expedition to Cadiz in 1596 (M.). Later bishop of Lincoln and London, and archbishop of York. Cf. p. 69. See *DNB* ('Montaigne').

Laelia] Fuller's *History of Cambridge* dated the production of *Laelia* as 1597–8, when Essex visited Cambridge as Chancellor of the University. G. C. Moore Smith (*The Cambridge Play 'Laelia'* (1911)) argued that the correct date is 1 March 1595.

iv.20] Dudley North (1581–1666), eldest son of Sir John North, in 1600 succeeded his grandfather as Lord North. Fellow Commoner, Trinity, *c.* 1597, but left without a degree. Author and musician. Died 1667. (See *DNB*).

iv.21] Rudio: (?) Robert Rudd, sizar at Queens', 1582; BA, 1585–6; MA, 1590; BD, 1597; Fellow, 1589–1600; or (?) Anthony Rudd, pensioner at Queens', Lent, 1597–8.

iv.22] For Weever's sonnet to Shakespeare see pp. 90–92. There are at least three misprints here; read 'rosy-tinted' (l. 3), 'Rose-cheek'd' (l. 5), 'Romeo' (l. 9). 'Honey-tongued' is also Meres' epithet for Shakespeare; *OED* records it first in *Love's Labour's Lost*, but 'honey-mouthed' dates from 1539. 'Rose-cheek'd Adonis' comes from *Venus and Adonis*, l. 3, as does 'fire-hot Venus' ('She red and hot as coals of glowing fire', l. 35). Weever re-used 'power attractiue beuty / subiectiue dutie' in *Faunus* (cf. p. 29, above). 'Het' in l. 13 'means "heated"' (M.).

iv.23 *Ed: Allen*] Edward Alleyn (1566–1626), the actor and son-in-law of Philip Henslowe (who had an interest in the Swan theatre). 'Swans' could refer to London's dramatists, or may be a misprint for Swan (so 'Meander' for Menander). See *DNB*.

v. *dedication*] Sir Thomas Gerard (*c.* 1564–1617), son of Sir Gilbert Gerard, was at Caius College, Cambridge (1580), became a JP in Lancs., Middlesex, Northants, Staffs., and knight marshal of the Household in 1597. See above, p. 69; Hasler; *Lost Years*, p. 158, n.3.

v.1] Sir Peter Leigh or Legh (c. 1563–1636) of Lyme, Cheshire, and Winwick, Lancs. Knighted 1599. See *Lost Years*, Hasler, and Lady Newton, *The House of Lyme* (1917).

v.4. *Iscus*] (?) John Isham, pensioner at Queens' (1597).

v.5. *Charis*] (?) John Grace, at St John's c. 1596 ('charin' = grace).

v.7. *Brundon*] There was a Robert Brundish at Peterhouse from c. 1593. Here Weever echoes *The Faerie Queene* (II.2.29): 'Vain is the vaunt, and victory unjust / That more to mighty hands than rightful cause doth trust' (see M.).

v.8. *Rubrio*] Cf. iv.17.

v.9] Cf. p. 10, above, and G. C. Williamson, *George, Third Earl of Cumberland (1558–1605)* (Cambridge, 1920). The Earl was the queen's Champion, and a notable voyager. One of his ships was called the *Malice Scourge* or simply the *Scourge* (Williamson, pp. 142, 147).

v.10] Nathaniel Fletcher: Fellow of Queens' (1594–1611), and elder brother of the dramatist, John Fletcher. Son of Richard Fletcher, Bishop of London (d. 1596).

v.12. *Otho*] (?) John Otter (Corpus, 1596) or G. Otway (Christ's, 1596–7).

v.13. *Galbus*] (?) Henry Gale (sizar at Corpus, c. 1593; BA from Queens', 1596–7).

v.14. *Pontus*] (?) John Seaman, Fellow of Queens' (1583–94), or Paul Seaman (pensioner at Queens', 1591).

v.15. *Naevius*] (?) Christopher Nevell (Fellow Commoner at Queens', 1594), who was 'doubtless 3rd son of Edward, Lord Abergavenny' (Venn).

v.16] Thomas Holcroft, Esq., of Vale Royal, Cheshire (1557–1620), knighted 1603. His sister married the third Earl of Rutland (see above, p. 9, and i.13). In Hasler.

v.18] 'Beloe points out that this epigram ... is from the Latin of Michael Tarcagnota Marullus (d. 1500). See M. T. Marullus etc., *Poetae elegantissimi*, Speyer, 1595, p. 26' (M.).

v.19] T. Foxe, W. Foxcroft, J. and T. Foxley were contemporaries of Weever at Cambridge. The last two were at Emmanuel, a 'Puritan' college.

v.21. *Sippus*] (?) Robert Gustard

(Trinity, c. 1595); 'to sip' = degustare. Or Richard Sibbes (sizar, St John's, c. 1594)?

v.22] There was a Gabriel Grant at Trinity from c. 1593. Perhaps Weever wrote 'G.', which was wrongly expanded?

v.23] Probably John Egerton, first Earl of Bridgewater (1579–1649), second son of Lord Chancellor Ellesmere and his father's heir after the death of his brother Thomas (cf. vii.11). Both brothers served in Ireland in 1599. Milton wrote *Comus* for Egerton's family. See *DNB*.

v.24] Henry Porter, vicar of Lancaster (1582–1600), knew the family of Henry Butler, Weever's uncle (see DDF 951, a letter of attorney, 1594). Cf. Hall, *Poems*, p. 19: 'mell not with holy things'.

vi, *dedication*] For Sir Cuthbert Halsall see *Lost Years*, p. 47. Knighted in Ireland, 1599. Sir Cuthbert's later debts can be traced in DDIn 47, 49, 55, 64, 69, etc.; his will (27 Feb. 1632) is in DDIn 44 (5). High Sheriff of Lancashire, 1601. Connected with Sir Richard Hoghton in many documents. His wife, Dorothy, was a daughter of the fourth Earl of Derby and a sister of Ursula Halsall, probably the phoenix of Shakespeare's *The Phoenix and the Turtle* (*Lost Years*, p. 90 ff.).

vi.1. *thy gold-gilded tower*] For Sir Richard's 'princely tower' see *Lost Years*, p. 8.

vi.3] See p. 6.

vi.4] William Hoghton was the second son of Thomas Hoghton (as in vi.3), and brother of Sir Richard (vi.1).

vi.6. *Sullus, Mat*] (?) Francis Salkeld, (pensioner, Queens', 1594) and Mathy Welbere (pensioner, Queens', 1595).

vi.7] As vi.8 refers to Bishop Jewel, vi.7 might possibly be about Dr Richard Cosin (Chancellor of Worcester, 1583; Dean of the Arches and Vicar-general of Canterbury; MP) who died Nov. 30 1597. W. Barlow's *Vita et obitus Richardi Cosin* (1598) included verses by Nathaniel Fletcher, and verses written 'rogatu Overalli' (pp. 56, 67–8; cf. above, v. 10, iii.23).

vi.8] John Jewel (1522–71), Bishop of Salisbury. In *DNB*.

vi.9] Ferdinando Stanley, the fifth Earl of Derby, died in April 1594; his death 'was rumoured to be due to witchcraft ...

which is alluded to in the next epigram' (M.). A patron of poets and actors: see *Lost Years*, p. 59 ff., *DNB*.

vi.11] Presumably Marston and Jonson were seen as friends when Weever bracketed their names together. This is a very early tribute to Marston, whose first satires appeared anonymously in 1598 (SR 27 May, 8 September).

vi.13] William Warner (1558?–1609) published *Albion's England* in 1586, and there were three other editions before 1599. Meres called this work 'absolute' (cf. p. 91, above), but so did Nashe in 1589, in the preface to *Menaphon* (M.). A friend of Drayton. In *DNB*.

vi.14] William Abraham (sizar, Clare, *c.* 1595) was buried at St Edward's Church, Cambridge, 9 Oct. 1596 (Venn).

vi.15] 'After its original issue in 1589 Peele's *Tale of Troy* was printed as a thumb-book, and an edition dated 1604, measuring about 1½ inches high, has been preserved' (M.).

vi.18] Could this refer to John Fisher, perhaps the most famous President of Queens' (1505–8)? He was also bishop of Rochester, and was executed in 1535 for denying the king's supremacy. But I have not traced the incident referred to.

vi.21] Cf. p. 14. Probably refers to Thomas Cook (St John's, 1582; BA, 1585–6; Fellow, 1586; Proctor, 1595); vi.22 also refers to a proctor.

vi.22] William Rich, pensioner of Pembroke Hall, 1583; BA, 1586–7; Fellow, 1588; Proctor, 1598–9.

vi.23] Spenser died in January, 1599. 'This epigram is the authority for thinking that the *Ruins of Time* volume was called in' (M.); 'called in' meant suppressed.

vi.24] James Thornton was rector of Halton, Lancs, 1591–1605 (Venn). A clergyman is probably meant; William Hulton of Hulton, Esq. (or Halton of Halton) was a close friend of the Hoghtons (*Lost Years*, pp. 20, 28, 142) and of the Daltons of Pilling, so the rector of Halton is probably Weever's 'well read' friend. Cf. p. 8.

vi.25] Edward was probably related to John Wrightington, Esq., of Wrightington, Lancs., a deputy lieutenant and JP. 'The family was not Heraldic, and never appeared at the Lancashire Visitations' (*The Stanley*

Papers, Part II (*CS*, xxxi, 1853, p. 120).

vii, *dedication*] Cf. v.1.

vii.1] Cf. v, dedication.

vii.2] Carus may be a student called Carr (cf. ii.8).

vii.3] (?) Samuel Sparke (sizar, Emmanuel, 1594); or 'Sparsus' from 'spargo' (strew)—(?) Richard Strode (St John's, 1597–8). 'Pretour' is not in *OED*, but could be from French *prêteur*, a lender.

vii.4] Cf. v.14.

vii.5, 6] (?) Four Trinity men—T. Hughes (BA, 1598–9; H. Chipperfield (sizar from *c.* 1596); S. Claiton (sizar from *c.* 1594); and either J. Wood (sizar from *c.* 1597) or S. Bush (sizar from *c.* 1596).

vii.7. *Lacus*] (?) Hugh Lake (sizar, St John's, *c.* 1595).

vii.8. *Portian*] (?) G. Porter (pensioner, Queens', 1593).

Grillus] (?) S. Cricke (sizar, Trinity, *c.* 1596) or E. Hopkins (sizar, Trinity, *c.* 1596); 'grillus' = cricket, grasshopper.

vii.9] 'In old time we had treen chalices and golden priests, but now we have treen priests and golden chalices' (Bishop J. Jewel, *Certain Sermons*, ed. 1609, p. 176, cited in *The Oxford Dictionary of Quotations*; so also St Boniface the Martyr, quoted McKerrow. For Jewel see vi.8).

vii.10. *Cacus*] (?) Francis Cacott (pensioner, Corpus, *c.* 1593) or John Cacott (pensioner, Trinity, 1593).

vii.11] Sir Thomas Egerton, son and heir of Lord Chancellor Ellesmere, was a Colonel in the Irish campaign (HMC, *Hatfield*, viii, 344), and was killed in August 1599. See p. 10, and v.23 note.

vii.12] Cf. Martial, iv.72: 'You beg me, Quintus, to present you my works. I have not a copy, but the bookseller Trypho has ... '

vii.13] Tubrio: see A6b, and Marston, *Poems*, pp. 223–6.

vii.14] 'Cordred' looks like word-play (cord-red, i.e. hangman?). Perhaps R. Stringer (sizar, Trinity, *c.* 1592; BA, 1596–7).

Saint Fooles, Steeple faire] Cf. Hall, *Poems*, p. 28 (M., with other examples.).

vii.17] Martial, trying to outflank criticism in 'To the Reader' (Book 1), also compared himself with Pedo and Getulicus.

NOTES

I. INTRODUCTION

1 See p. 83.
2 The Roxburghe Club reprinted *The Mirror of Martyrs* in 1873, with a short introduction by H. H. Gibbs, but without notes.

II. FAMILY CONNECTIONS IN LANCASHIRE

1 See *Lost Years*, Ch. 5: 'John Weever and the Hoghtons'.
2 G. J. Piccope, *Lancashire and Cheshire Wills*, third portion (CS, 1861, p. 182).
3 Henry Fishwick, *The History of the Parish of St Michaels-on-Wyre* (CS, 1891, p. 151).
4 *Funeral Monuments*, pp. 50, 288, 103 (misprinted 104).
5 Fishwick, p. 153.
6 PRO, DL7.26.36.
7 PRO, Duchy of Lancaster, Special Commissions, no. 426 (30 Elizabeth).
8 'A note of such legacies as were given and bequeathed by Anne Butler late of Rawcliffe', 1622 (LRO).
9 Quoted by Fishwick, p. 149.
10 See *Lost Years*, p. 13.
11 BL, Add. MS. 32, 106, fo. 206 ff. This is a copy of the Earl of Derby's report, dated 7 January 1590. It states that Thomas Hoghton and Richard Baldwin were killed, 'but by whom is not yet known'. The participants in the riot, including 'Johne Weyver', are named.
12 Library of the Society of Antiquaries, MS. 127, fos. 180a, 149b.
13 John G. A. Prim, *Memorials of the Family of Langton of Kilkenny* (Dublin, 1864), p. 12; Edward Baines, *Duchy of Lancaster* (5 vols., 1888), IV, 382.
14 PRO, C2 JAS1. H34.43.
15 Hasler, 'Thomas Langton'.
16 George C. Miller, *Hoghton Tower* (Preston, 1948), p. 162.
17 *Lost Years*, pp. 20–21.
18 See *Lost Years*, p. 151.
19 See *Epigrammes*, iv.15, note.

III. CAMBRIDGE

1 I give more particulars in the notes on the epigrams concerned.
2 Chambers, *Shakespeare*, I, 360.
3 See below, p. 52.
4 Martial, i.18; ii.19; iii.13, etc.
5 Iscus, of course, also recalls Martial's Nasica: 'You invite me then, and then only, Nasica, when you know I am engaged ... ' (ii.79).
6 John Strype, *John Whitgift* (1718), p. 481.
7 P. 103 (misprinted 104).
8 *Lost Years*, pp. 15–30, etc.

IV. EARLY YEARS IN LONDON

1 McKerrow, p. vi.
2 Cf. p. 59.
3 Newdigate, pp. 98–9.
4 See Franklin B. Williams, Jr., *Index of Dedications and Commendatory Verses in English Books Before 1641* (The Bibliographical Society, 1962).
5 Newdigate, p. 97. (NB: Newdigate confused the first two book-titles: cf. above, p. 26 .)
6 Ferguson, p. 5.
7 *Ibid.*, p. 86.
8 See note 6.
9 Ferguson, pp. 7–8.
10 *Ibid.*, p. 13.
11 *Ibid.*, p. 9.
12 *Ibid.*, p. 17.
13 A. W. Pollard, *Shakespeare's Fight with the Pirates* (Cambridge, ed. 1937, p. 48). S. Thomas, however, has challenged this view of Burbie (*Sh.Q.*, 1976, 27, 186 ff.).
14 *DNB*, 'Francis Meres'.
15 Newdigate, p. 97.
16 McKerrow, p. v.
17 Crawford, p. 388.
18 Davenport later corrected the oversight in *The Whipper Pamphlets*, II, 63.
19 Crawford, p. viii.
20 P. 506.
21 P. xxix.
22 *Faunus*, p. v.
23 *Ibid.*, p. vi.
24 Crawford, no. 38.
25 The *Short Title Catalogue* (1926) dated the SR entry of *Mirror* 11 August 1601, but this was the entry for Munday and Drayton's *Oldcastle* play. (*STC*, 2nd edn., 1976, gives no SR entry for *Mirror*, correctly.)
26 Searle, p. 389.
27 David B. McKeen, 'A Memory of Honour' *A Study of the House of Cobham of Kent* (Birmingham PhD thesis, 1964), pp. 942–3. I am grateful for permission to consult the late Dr McKeen's typescript, which is shortly to be published.
28 Society of Antiquaries, MS. 127, fo. 83b.
29 *The Mirror of Martyrs*, B5.
30 See L. M. Oliver, 'Sir Thomas Oldcastle: Legend or Literature?' (*The Library*, 5th series, 1947, I, 179–83); Bale, G2b ff.
31 As in note 30.
32 Also noted by McKeen, p. 989.
33 Lambard, pp. 392–3; Weever, B4b.
34 Compare p. 33 (Weever's allusion to *Julius Caesar*), and pp. 3, 90.
35 Ferguson, p. 20.
36 A. Davenport, *The Whipping of the Satyre*, p. v. Compare Davenport's explanation of *Faunus*, quoted p. 30.
37 *Faunus*, p. viii.
38 Davenport, *The Collected Poems of Joseph Hall* (1949), p. xviii, n.2.
39 Chambers, *Elizabethan Stage*, III, 366.
40 See *The Whipper Pamphlets*, II, 40–45; also below, p. 42, for Weever's smallness.

V. SATIRICAL PORTRAITS OF WEEVER IN ENGLISH PLAYS, 1598–1601

1 Chambers, *Elizabethan Stage*, III, 293.

2 *Party par pale*: 'a term in heraldry denoting that the field or ground on which the figures that make up a coat of arms are represented, is divided into two equal parts ... [Marston] means that the external appearances of the two sexes are, in Simplicius, divided with equal exactness' (Dilke, quoted in Marston, *Plays*, II, 347–8).

3 Marston, *Plays*, II, 246 (spelling modernised).

4 *Ibid.*, II, 286, 256, 257.

5 *Ibid.*, II, 251.

6 *Dekker*, I, 321, 318.

7 *Jonson* (Everyman), I, 60, 103.

8 *Ibid.*, I, 98, 116–17.

9 *Ibid.*, I, 116.

10 *Ibid.*, I, 98, 119–21, 134, 140.

11 Compare p. 48, above.

12 *Dekker*, I, 357; *Jonson* (Everyman), I, 120, 134–5, 103.

13 L. 127 ff.

14 *Jonson* (Oxford), VIII, 32.

15 *Jonson* (Everyman), I, 28.

16 *Dekker*, I, 351.

17 *Faunus*, pp. 67–8.

18 For the dates of these plays see Chambers, *Elizabethan Stage*, and Honigmann, 'The Date and Revision of *Troilus and Cressida*' (in J. J. McGann, ed., *Textual Criticism and Literary Interpretation*, (1985, pp. 38–54).

19 *A Shakespeare Encyclopaedia*, p. 871.

20 Weever's friend, Michael Drayton, published a satirical poem called *The Owl* in 1604, in which 'the harmless owl' (l. 200) is set upon by other birds because it has exposed their Vices. This impenetrable poem is thought to have been begun before the death of Queen Elizabeth, and caused a stir when it appeared (Newdigate, pp. 130–32).

21 Presumably it was the dwarfish actor who was 'thin-faced'. In the only surviving likeness of John Weever, which dates from thirty years later, his face was not noticeably thin.

22 *Parnassus Plays*, p. 182.

23 *Ibid.*, p. 126.

24 *Ibid.*, p. 143. My italics.

25 *Ibid.*, p. 143, note.

26 P. 153.

27 P. 178 ff.

28 *Epigrammes*, v.6. Others (e.g. Sir Edward Dyer) had written in praise of nothing (cf. also McKerrow's *Nashe*, III, 177), but Weever's interest in epigrams and epitaphs, already visible in his first book, suggests that he is the target here.

29 *Parnassus Plays*, p. 71 ff.

30 P. 146.

31 P. 155. Some of those addressed in Weever's *Epigrammes* were gentlemen in Lancashire, etc., who owned extensive estates, including many farms.

32 P. 181.

33 Pp. 146, 177.

34 P. 183 ff.

35 See *Epigrammes*, i.16, 19–20; ii.21, and notes, and *Parnassus Plays*, p. 256.

36 We have to postulate a composite portrait, or that Ingenioso is someone other than Nashe

in *The Return*, Part 2, because Ingenioso and a friend speak of Nashe as deceased in this play (cf. *Parnassus Plays*, pp. 79 and 245).
37 F. L. Huntley, *Bishop Joseph Hall* (Cambridge, 1979), p. 30.
38 Sigs. E4b–E5a.
39 *Parnassus Plays*, p. 41.

VI. FROM 1601 TO 1631

1 *The History of Clerkenwell*, by W. J. Pinks (ed. E. J. Wood, 1881), p. 90.
2 Cf. p. 8.
3 John G. A. Prim, *Memorials of the Family of Langton of Kilkenny* (Dublin, 1864), p. 12.
4 Hasler, II, 439.
5 Cf. p. 1.
6 PRO, C2 JAS1 B40.30.
7 See the will of John Onion, alias Divell, collier, 1629 (PCC).
8 Society of Antiquaries, MS. 127, fo. 203.
9 *Ibid.*, fo. 202b.
10 *Downshire Manuscripts* (HMC), II (1936), 214.
11 See also below, p. 61.
12 See also Nicholas H. Nicolas, *Memoir of Augustine Vincent* (1827).
13 Society of Antiquaries, MS. 128, fo. 98b.
14 Joan Evans, *A History of the Society of Antiquaries* (Oxford, 1956), p. 8. In this paragraph I am indebted to Evans, Ch. I: 'Antiquarianism in the English Renaissance'. See also F. J. Levy, *Tudor Historical Thought* (San Marino, 1967).
15 Evans, pp. 10–11.
16 Society of Antiquaries, MS. 127, fo. 176b.
17 Society of Antiquaries, MS. 128, fo. 379a. I have modernised the spelling. The first line has several deletions (including *high* and *durst*) and, presumably, was intended as 'He whose undaunted spirit did out-face'.
18 *Lost Years*, p. 58.
19 Compare *Hamlet*: 'now go to my Ladies chamber, and *bid her paint* her selfe an inch thicke, *to this she must come*' (first Quarto); 'Now get you to my Ladies table, & tell her, *let her paint* an inch thicke, *to this fauour she must come*' (second Quarto). (My italics.)

VII. *ANCIENT FUNERAL MONUMENTS*

1 Society of Antiquaries, MS. 127, fo. 121a.
2 See *Lost Years*, p. 80.
3 Society of Antiquaries, MS. 128, fo. 382b.
4 Dugdale, of course, took an interest in such matters. He recorded that 'one Gerard Johnson' made Shakespeare's tomb, an attribution now generally accepted (Chambers, *Shakespeare*, II, 183).
5 Chambers, *Shakespeare*, II, 181.
6 See p. 90.
7 BL, Lansdowne MS.874, fo.15a.
8 Society of Antiquaries, MS. 127, fo. 104a.
9 MS. 127, fo. 233b.
10 *Funeral Monuments*, pp. 531, 651, 686.
11 *Ibid.*, pp. 273, 500, 864.
12 In one copy in the British Library, G 773, there is a handwritten note that 'the rarity of this

book in Large Paper is sufficiently known. In this Copy, which is the finest that I ever saw, the Index also is in L.P. but in almost all the other copies, the Index is on small paper, & is inlaid to match the body of the book.'

VIII. DEATH AND MONUMENT

1 The original wills of John and Anne Weever are in the PRO (PCC); I have modernised spelling and punctuation. In *Lost Years* I reproduced John Weever's will from a contemporary copy (also in the PRO): this accounts for some very minor differences.
2 I have come across only one other John and Anne 'Weaver' of London. Anne Wardeley, executrix of 'John Weaver, her late husband, deceased', filed a bill of complaint in the Court of Requests in 1602 (Req. 2, 283/20).
3 Cf. p. 2.
4 Baines, *Duchy of Lancaster* (4 vols., 1836), IV, 400.
5 Evans, p. 192.
6 Cf. p. 82.
7 *Funeral Monuments*, p. 1.

APPENDIX

1 I hear from the Bodleian Library that 'A7 appears to have been tipped in', and from Harvard's Houghton Library that, in the Harvard copy, there is no certain evidence one way or the other: it cannot be proved that A7 'was tipped in or is a cancel'.
2 McKerrow, pp. vi–vii.
3 *Lost Years*, pp. 55–6.
4 Ferguson, p. 25. For Simmes's compositors see also Ferguson, *Studies in Bibliography*, 1960, XIII, 19–29; Alan E. Craven, *SB*, 1973, XXVI, 37–60; MacD. P. Jackson, *SB*, 1982, XXXV, 173–90.
5 See note on iv.3.
6 *Lost Years*, p. 54.
7 See Chambers, *Shakespeare*, II, 218.
8 See also *Epigrammes*, vi.13, note.
9 See also *Lost Years*, p. 29.

INDEX